MW01070475

To Heather ありがとう:

Naomi Yamamoto

Feb 2020

SUGAR
FLOWERS

THE SIGNATURE COLLECTION

Photography by Takeharu Hioki

NAOMI YAMAMOTO

First published in October 2018
by B. Dutton Publishing Limited,
The Grange, Hones Yard, Farnham,
Surrey, GU9 8BB, UK.
Reprinted in January 2019.

Copyright: Naomi Yamamoto 2018

ISBN-13: 978-1-905113-57-6

All rights reserved.

No part of this publication may be reproduced,
stored in a retrieval system or transmitted in any
form or by means electronic, mechanical,
photocopying, recording, or otherwise, without
prior written permission of the copyright owner. A
catalogue record of this book is available from the
British Library.

Naomi Yamamoto has asserted her right under the
Copyright, Designs and Patents Act, 1988, to be
identified as the author of this work.

Printed and bound in Turkey by Imago Publishing Limited

Publisher: Beverley Dutton

Editor-in-Chief: Jenny Weaver

Creative Director: Sarah Ryan

Commissioning Editor: Jennifer Kelly

Copy Editors: Adele Duthie, Emily Gussin

Photography: Takeharu Hioki

Horticultural Expert: Alan Titchmarsh

Disclaimer

The Author and Publisher have made every effort to ensure that the
contents of this book, if followed carefully, will not cause harm or injury
or pose any danger. Please note that some inedible items, such as floral
wires, have been used in the projects in this book. All such inedible
items must be removed from a cake before it is eaten. Similarly, any
equipment and substances not approved for contact with food, such as
non-toxic glue, must not come into contact with anything that is to be
eaten. Neither the Author nor the Publisher can be held responsible for
errors or omissions and cannot accept liability for injury, damage or loss
to persons or property, however it may arise, as a result of acting upon
guidelines and information printed in this book.

ACKNOWLEDGEMENTS

First and foremost, I would like to express my
gratitude to Beverley and Robert Dutton. They
have continuously supported me ever since
Squires Kitchen Magazine Publishing first
published *Wedding Cakes – A Design Source* in
1999 and I contributed to this magazine. They
gave me the chance to teach at Squires Kitchen
International School, publish my first book
written in English, *Wedding Cakes: The Couture
Collection*, and be a co-author in the award-
winning title *The Art of Sugarcraft*. Now this
book, *Sugar Flowers: The Signature Collection*,
is being released. I feel very privileged and will
always be grateful to them.

I would like to thank the publishing team, the
excellent editors Jenny Weaver and Adele Duthie
and the extremely talented designer Sarah Ryan,
for their hard work in putting the book together
so beautifully.

I also would like to say a big thank you to editor
Sachiko Iinuma and Takeharu Hioki, a foremost
photographer in Japan. Sachiko gave me
precious technical advice and helped with the
settings over the course of eighteen months
when the photography took place.

And finally, I would like to thank my family,
especially my daughter Seiko who is my best
adviser for writing in English and managing
stress. They are, and always will be, my
greatest supporters.

SUGAR
FLOWERS
THE SIGNATURE COLLECTION

MASTER FIVE SIMPLE FLOWERS,
CREATE COUNTLESS STUNNING VARIETIES

Introduction

In all of the work I have created since I first started sugarcrafting, it is my sugar flowers that attract the most attention.

When creating this book, I gave thought to the kind of flowers I make and what cake decorators want to see the most. I came up with the idea to focus on five flowers, gorgeous like heroines of the stage and screen, popular and loved all over the world: the rose, lily, dahlia, tulip and peony.

In recent years there has been significant development of new breeds of flowers, such as David Austin's English roses. Flowers have become larger and shapes have evolved. This book brings together 25 varieties selected from the best of the five focal flowers. The step-by-step instructions and detailed photography reveal the process behind giving sugar flowers a natural look from start to finish to make sure that anyone can make them. My signature tips and techniques for finishing flowers beautifully and realistically appear throughout the book.

Creating sugar flowers requires repetitive and skilful work, making petals and leaves one by one before bringing them together in one flower. It is very time-consuming and much patience is needed. While the time and the effort are paid off by the wonderful end result, for this book I wanted to find a way to work as efficiently as possible and finish flowers just as beautifully. After much trial and error, I found that the secret was knowing how to use key tools to make a number of different petals and leaves for sugar flowers.

As a result, I created three sets of cutters with Squires Kitchen. The cutters can be used for a wide variety of petals and leaves as most of them are based on one of three shapes – round, teardrop and almond – and they can also be used to further modify each shape. SK Multi-Flower Cutter Sets are used to create all 25 flowers in this book. If you already own cutters of a similar size and shape, I recommend that you use them. If not, I hope that these new cutter sets prove to be the perfect tools for you.

When it comes to turning a flat cut-out into a three-dimensional, natural shape, you don't need lots of different sugarcraft tools: simple bamboo skewers and polystyrene balls are used for many of the flowers in this book. The foundation techniques I introduce are also applicable to countless other blooms; I would be delighted if you use them to add your own twist to your sugar flower creations.

In nature, flowers and leaves vary widely while maintaining the key features which identify them. I recommend focusing on what makes a certain flower attractive rather than making them uniform. By using just your hands and a few key tools, and by giving beautiful colour and expression to petals and leaves, you will create unique and wonderful flowers.

I am sincerely grateful to be able to produce *Sugar Flowers: The Signature Collection* with B. Dutton Publishing. I hope this book helps make your sugarcraft life enjoyable and inspires you as much as I was inspired by the books of my predecessors.

Naomi

Contents

By using just your hands and a few key tools, and by giving beautiful colour and expression to petals and leaves, you will create unique and wonderful flowers.

122	128	134	140	146
Semi-Cactus Dahlia	Collarette Dahlia	Anemone-Flowered Dahlia	Tulip Foundations	Single Late Tulip
152	156	162	166	172
Lily-Flowered Tulip	Parrot Tulip	Fringed Tulip	Double-Flowered Tulip	Peony Foundations
180	186	194	200	206
Chinese Peony	Anemone Peony	Peony Rose	Cupped Double Peony	Temari Peony

Author Profile

Naomi Yamamoto is a well-respected sugar artist, wedding cake designer and instructor who has been teaching her specialist techniques for over 30 years. Her work is elegant, meticulous, shows a high level of creativity and draws recognition not only in Japan but also from enthusiasts worldwide, particularly her beautiful sugar flowers.

My sugarcraft career is a result of two important elements: a passion inherited from my mother, and some lucky encounters in my life.

My mother was a keen painter; she was especially good at portraits in a style influenced by French artist, Edgar Degas. When I was a little girl, the house was full of her paintings and other artistic works such as elaborate embroidery and knitted designs. I was her little daughter who loved flowers. I have always liked decorating with flowers so it is no wonder that cake decorating attracts me so much.

I made my first decorated cake soon after getting married, when my daughter was still little. My favourite hobby was to bake cakes for celebrations and I was always curious about how to decorate cakes beautifully to make them look really special. At that time in Japan, there were no decorated cakes or cake decorating lessons, so when my family moved to the US for three years it was a chance for me to learn how to decorate cakes. When my daughter had her second birthday party, I made a tall two-tier birthday cake decorated in pink with an elephant on top – it was a lovely moment.

After our return to Japan, people who were interested in sugarcraft came to my home to have private lessons. Meanwhile, I returned to the US and travelled to England to learn sugarcraft professionally. My students and I held exhibitions in Japan and sugarcraft started to appear in the media.

One of the most important moments in my career happened in 1985 when Meiji Kinenkan, the prestigious wedding ceremony company, contacted me. Known for being the wedding company for the Japanese royal family, they had a new sugarcraft school project. In the early 80s, the royal wedding of the Prince of Wales and Lady Diana Spencer in England was big news in Japan, and their beautifully decorated wedding cake had caught the attention of Japanese people. It was the

Naomi teaching at Squires Kitchen International School

start of a busy career as an executive instructor at the Genteel Academy of Meiji Kinenkan in Tokyo, where I taught sugarcraft for 13 years. Little by little, sugarcraft came to be well-known throughout Japan.

Another significant connection for me was with Beverley Dutton, Managing Director of Squires Kitchen. When Squires Kitchen first published *Wedding Cakes – A Design Source* magazine in 1999, I submitted photos of my work. Beverley kindly included them in the following issues and my creations featured on three front covers. My work started to appear in Japanese media, including TV, as well as international media such as *Cakes & Sugarcraft* magazine. I have since demonstrated and acted as a judge at high-profile sugarcraft events around the world including the Japan Cake Show, the Squires Kitchen Exhibition and the British Sugarcraft Guild's International Exhibition in the UK, BCN&CAKE in Spain and the São Paulo Sugarcraft Show in Brazil.

My first book, *Delicate Sugarcraft from Japan*, was published by Shibata Shoten in August 2007. It was a big project which I started at the same time as teaching at the Genteel Academy. Although it is in Japanese, it has become a favourite with sugarcrafters all over the world thanks to the detailed step-by-step photography. In March 2013, my first book in English, *Wedding Cakes: The Couture Collection*, was published by B. Dutton Publishing, followed by *The Art of Sugarcraft* in March 2014, a collaborative book by Squires Kitchen International School tutors and winner of the Best UK Food Book for Professionals in the 2014 Gourmand World Cookbook Awards. It was truly an honour for me to be a part of both books and I am deeply appreciative of the hard work by everyone involved.

I currently teach sugarcraft at Squires Kitchen International School in the UK, at the Japan Confectionery School in Tokyo and at many other schools around the world. Students also come from overseas to my atelier in Tokyo to have private lessons. I would like to send my sincere thanks to all the motivated international students whom I have met. It makes me happy to think of so many young, passionate students actively working on sugarcraft in their home countries.

Naomi with Carlos Lischetti on the SK stand at Bakery China, 2018.

Launch of *The Art of Sugarcraft* (B. Dutton Publishing)

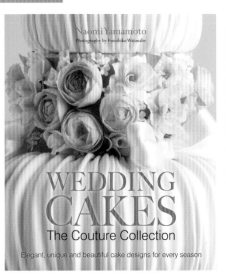

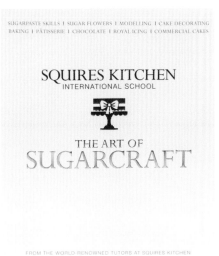

ESSENTIAL EDIBLES AND EQUIPMENT
for Making Sugar Flowers

You will need the same basic items to make most of the sugar flowers in this book, so if you make flowers regularly it is worth investing in any items that you don't already have. I have included a description of each item so if you are new to flower making this should help you get started.

Any specific requirements for edibles and equipment are listed at the beginning of the method for each flower so you can make sure you have everything you need before you begin. All of the items are readily available from sugarcraft suppliers, see page 216.

EDIBLES

Sugar flowers are generally made from edible products to ensure they are safe to display on celebration cakes. Make sure the recipient is aware that sugar flowers shouldn't be consumed if they are made with any inedible items such as stamens, wires or non-food-safe glazes. If you are making flowers for a cake, always remove them before cutting the cake.

Flower Paste (Sugar Florist Paste/SFP)

Also known as gumpaste, flower paste contains gum tragacanth or CMC which makes it strong enough to roll out very thinly without breaking. Gelatine can help to strengthen the paste as well.

There are many ready-to-use flower pastes available from sugarcraft suppliers, including Squires Kitchen Sugar Florist Paste (SFP). Because it is readymade, the recipe is always consistent and therefore more convenient to use. It also comes in many different colours, which is very useful for saving time when making sugar flowers and leaves.

If you would like to make your own flower paste, I have included a recipe opposite.

Flower Paste Recipe

When not in use, store the fresh paste in the refrigerator for up to one month and in the freezer for up to six months. Take only what you need from the refrigerator or freezer, allow the paste to come to room temperature and knead the paste to soften it before use. If you have added colour to paste for a project, keep it at room temperature and use within a week.

500g (1lb 1¾oz) icing sugar
18g (⅝oz) gum tragacanth or CMC
62g (2⅛oz) cooled, boiled water
8g (¼oz) powdered gelatine
10g (⅜oz) liquid glucose
50g (1¾oz) white vegetable fat, melted, plus extra for greasing

Makes 620g (1lb 5⅞oz)

1 Sift the icing sugar at least twice and place it in the ovenproof bowl of a food mixer. Add the gum tragacanth or CMC and cover the bowl with aluminium foil. Place it in the oven at a low heat or in a bain-marie for a few minutes until the sugar is warm.

2 Pour the cooled, boiled water into a bowl and sprinkle the gelatine on top. Leave it to soak according to the pack instructions.

3 Warm (but do not boil) the gelatine and water in a bain-marie to dissolve the gelatine completely. Remove from the heat, add the liquid glucose and mix well.

4 Add the gelatine and glucose mixture and the melted white vegetable fat to the warmed icing sugar. Beat them on a slow speed until they are well mixed then increase the speed and beat the mixture for a few minutes until it has a stringy texture.

5 Rub a little white vegetable fat on a non-stick rolling board. Remove the mixture from the bowl and knead it on the board. Divide the paste into approximately 10 pieces. Rub a little white vegetable fat into your palms and roll each piece into a ball. Wrap each ball tightly with cling film, place them in a food-grade polythene bag and seal the bag in an airtight container. Leave the sealed flower paste at room temperature for half a day before working with it.

If the flower paste is too soft, knead sifted icing sugar into it a little at a time until you reach the desired consistency. If the paste is too stiff, knead a small amount of white vegetable fat or edible glue into it.

Icing Sugar

All kinds of sugar pastes and royal icing are made mainly from icing sugar. Always sift icing sugar before use as it can form lumps in humid conditions. I prefer to use icing sugar rather than cornflour (corn starch/maize starch) to prevent paste from sticking to a board as cornflour can give the paste a rough texture.

Gum Tragacanth/CMC

Both gum tragacanth and CMC (carboxymethyl cellulose, also known as cellulose gum) give strength and pliability to sugar pastes. Gum tragacanth is natural product derived from the Astragalus gummifer tree and CMC is a food additive which gives a whiter finish to paste than gum tragacanth.

White Vegetable Fat

White vegetable fat prevents flower paste from sticking to the work surface and cutters. Lightly rub a very thin layer of fat onto the surface of the board and cutter before rolling out the paste.

Edible Glue

Edible glue is useful for sticking pieces of sugar work together before they dry out. Apply a tiny amount of edible glue with a fine paintbrush to the pieces you would like to stick together. Be careful not to use too much glue as the pieces could slide out of position and it may partially dissolve the paste. You can buy readymade edible glue from sugarcraft suppliers or make your own with the following recipe.

Edible Glue Recipe

1 Mix 15 parts cooled boiled water with 1 part gum tragacanth/CMC in a bowl. Cover the bowl and leave the mixture at room temperature for a day so the gum tragacanth/CMC has time to dissolve.

2 Store in a sterilised airtight container in the refrigerator for up to a week.

Paste Food Colours

Also known as gel colour, paste food colour is usually used for colouring flower paste and sugarpaste. See page 24 of Sugar Flower Foundations to find out more about colouring flower paste.

Dust Food Colours

Also known as powdered food colours, dust food colours are fine, edible powders. Brush them onto sugar petals and leaves to add depth of colour so they look more realistic. See page 24 of Sugar Flower Foundations to find out more about dusting sugar flowers.

Pollen Dust Food Colour

Pollen-style dust food colour has larger particles than standard dust food colours. It is useful for giving a realistic look to stamens as it adds both colour and texture: place the dust food colour in a small bowl, paint some edible glue on the anthers

then dip them into the colour. It can also be used for colouring the centres of sugar flowers.

Confectioners' Glaze

Confectioner's glaze is used to give a shiny finish to sugar leaves. Mix the glaze with clear alcohol, e.g. gin or vodka, before use for a less shiny result. Use glaze cleaner (isopropyl alcohol/IPA) to clean brushes after use.

EQUIPMENT

Please refer to Sugar Flower Foundations on pages 16–27 for more information on techniques for achieving different results using the following essential equipment.

Aluminium Foil and Tissue Paper

These are both useful for helping to maintain the shape of a petal, leaf or flower while it dries. Use tissue paper for petals and leaves, and aluminium foil for flowers.

Ball Tool

There are different sizes of ball tool: a larger one is useful for adding a wave to the edges of petals and for giving larger petals a shallow cupped form. I use a smaller ball tool for giving smaller petals a cup shape, and the smallest one for cupping tiny blossoms.

Bamboo Skewers

I often use a bamboo skewer for adding veins to a petal, rolling it along the paste on a non-stick board. It can also be used to curl the edges of a petal on a foam pad.

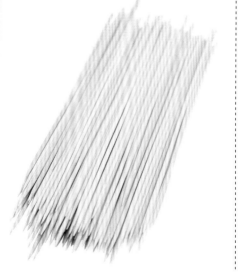

Bone Tool

A bone tool is useful for frilling the edges of any size of petal and for curling the tips of flower shapes with multiple petals such as daisies.

CelStick

These craft frilling sticks come in small, medium and large sizes; I find the medium one is the most useful for sugar flowers. You can roll out a small petal or leaf with a CelStick instead of a rolling pin, or use the rounded end to cup a multi-petal flower shape by pushing it into the centre on a foam pad. You can also make a small blossom by hollowing out the centre of a teardrop of paste with the pointed end and cutting out the petals with fine scissors.

Cocktail Sticks

Wooden cocktail sticks are useful throughout the process of making a sugar flower. Use the stick to take paste food colour from the bottle and add it to flower paste, or use it to curl the edge of a small petal. They can also be used for marking points on sugarpaste-covered cakes.

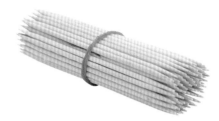

Cotton Thread

Cotton thread is used for making bunches of stamens. If you would like to shape the stamens, dip the bunch in egg white or edible glue and curve the threads with a cocktail stick as they firm up.

Cutters

There are cutters available for most types of flowers and leaves which make recreating the natural shapes quick and easy. If you are looking for a metal cutter, choose one made of stainless steel with a solid structure so it will not warp or go rusty.

Cutting Wheel

A cutting wheel is very useful as it allows you to cut out any size or shape of rolled-out paste on a non-stick board. The wheel is small and thin so it is easy to manoeuvre and the paste does not stick to it.

Fine, Pointed Scissors

I frequently use a small pair of scissors to make fine cuts in my sugar flower work. The finer the point of the blades, the easier they are to use.

Floral Tape

Floral tape has a papery, matt surface and is used to cover the wire stem of a sugar flower or leaf and to bind them together into arrangements. I also sometimes make calyces or leaves with the tape to prevent them from getting damaged. Green floral tape is the most useful colour and there are many others to choose from. See page 27 of Sugar Flower Foundations for more information on taping sugar flowers.

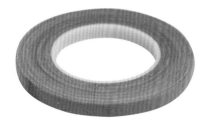

Floral Wire

Covered floral wires are used to give petals and leaves extra support. Usually white wire is used for a petal and green wire for a leaf. The higher

the gauge (width) number, the finer the wire. See page 18 of Sugar Flower Foundations for more information on choosing and using floral wires.

Flower/Leaf Shaping Tool

I use a tool with a flower shaper on one end (the wider end of the tool) and a leaf shaper on the thinner, pointed end. The flower shaping tool is used for thinning the edges of a petal or leaf. The leaf shaping tool is useful for creating veins and curling or curving a petal or leaf.

Foam Pad

Work on a food-grade foam pad when using tools to shape a petal or leaf. If you use tools to shape flower paste on a hard surface like a non-stick board, it will damage the petal or leaf. Some foam pads have holes in which are useful for shaping flowers and calyces made using the Mexican hat technique.

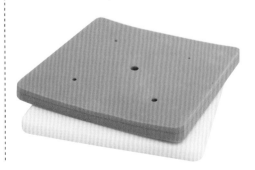

Non-stick Rolling Board and Pin

A non-stick board and a small, non-stick rolling pin are essential for rolling out flower paste smoothly and thinly. The boards are available in different sizes and some have grooves within them to create ridges in the paste for wired petals and leaves; this type of board can also be turned over and used as a flat, non-stick surface. Place a non-slip mat under the board before you roll out paste. I use a 15cm (6") long pin as it is the most useful size for making sugar flowers and leaves.

Paintbrushes

It is helpful to have a range of good-quality, food-safe brushes in different sizes. For edible glue, use a small brush for precision. When dusting colour onto a petal or a leaf, I recommend using a cosmetic brush reserved solely for sugarcraft as it has lots of fine hairs and holds more dust colour for better results. For dusting colour onto the edges of petals and leaves, use a flat brush held at a right angle to the edge. For painting, use a fine brush.

Paint Palette

A food-safe plastic paint palette with multiple wells allows you to keep dust food colours separate, mix them together and mix them with alcohol to make a paint, all in the same palette.

Petal and Leaf Veiners

Moulded veiners are the best way to recreate the natural veins found in petals and leaves, especially those with complex veins. Available in either one piece or as double-sided veiners, they are used to emboss the surface of the flower paste. You can find a wide range of specially designed veiners in sugarcraft shops; among them, double-sided veiners are the most effective ones for creating a realistic finish as they vein the front and back of the petal or leaf.

Polystyrene Bases and Formers

Polystyrene is my recommended base for sugar flowers as it is lighter than flower paste. Small balls, bud shapes and egg shapes can be used as the bases for flowers and buds, and ball shapes in different sizes are useful for keeping petals in a cupped form while they dry.

Small Palette Knife

This is useful for picking up a thin petal or leaf from a non-stick board without warping the shape.

Stamens

There are several varieties of stamens but seed-headed stamens are the most useful for sugar flowers. They come in double-ended bunches, so you will need to fold or cut them in half before attaching them around a flower paste pistil using floral tape.

Tweezers and Pliers

Angle-pointed tweezers and flat-nose pliers are essential tools for sugar flower arrangement. Use them to bend wire stems; it can sometimes be hard to do this with just your hands without knocking the delicate petals and leaves. I often use flat-nose pliers to manipulate a pistil and stamens.

Veining Tool

This tool has a textured end which you can roll over petals and leaves to created a veined effect. It is especially suited to flowers with complex veins such as roses.

Wire Cutters

Use wire cutters to cut floral wires; trimming wires with scissors can blunt them.

Cleaning Sugar Flower Equipment

If you use colours with the equipment, clean them by washing with hand soap as the colour will not be removed by neutral detergent. For boards, rolling pins and tools, soak a kitchen sponge with warm water, apply hand soap to the sponge and use it to wash the equipment. For paintbrushes, apply the soap to your hands and rub the bristles gently with your fingers. To rinse the brushes, swirl them in a bowl or cup of warm water.

Sugar Flower Foundations

CUTTING OUT PETALS AND LEAVES

There are numerous specially designed cutters available from sugarcraft shops. In this book, I only use SK Multi-Flower Cutter Sets. You can use SK Multi-Flower Cutter Sets 1, 2 and 3 to make many different types of petals and leaves as most of them are based on one of three shapes: round, teardrop or almond-shaped. These cutters make it quick and easy to form the basic shapes, which can then be customised for specific flowers with sugar tools.

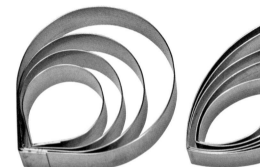

Preparing the Flower Paste

Place a non-slip mat underneath a non-stick board. Lightly grease the board with white vegetable fat and thinly roll out some Sugar Florist Paste (SFP) with a non-stick rolling pin or a CelStick.

Single Petal or Leaf Cutters

Cut out the petals or leaves using either a cutter or a cutting wheel with a template. For a neat cut, lightly grease the cutter with white vegetable fat. Place the cutter on the rolled-out paste, press down and, using small movements, slightly move the cutter one way and then the other to ensure a clean cut. Hold the cutter against the board and remove the paste around the cutter to leave a clean shape on the board.

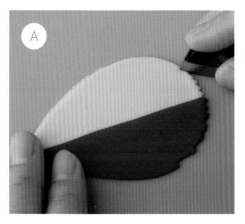

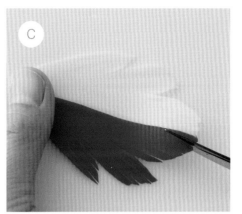

There are several ways to customise the cut-out shape of a petal: use the pointed end of a cutter for cutting out a small notch (A); use a cutting wheel to cut out a curve or a deep cut (B); and use fine scissors to make deep, narrow cuts (C).

Flower Cutters with Multiple Petals

When using a cutter with several petals, like a sunflower cutter, place the rolled-out SFP over the cutter and roll over it with a rolling pin to cut out the shape. This method is easier than pressing the cutter onto the paste and will cut the petals more cleanly.

Mexican Hat Technique

The Mexican hat technique is useful for making the basic shape of small, deep flowers or calyces.

1 Press a flattened ball of SFP against a hole in a food-grade foam pad to make a cone in the centre.

2 Remove the paste from the foam pad and place it on a non-stick board with the cone facing upwards. Use a CelStick to roll out the paste around the cone, then cut out the shape. Shape the petals or sepals as described in the specific flower instructions (D).

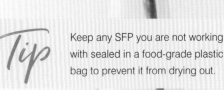

Tip Keep any SFP you are not working with sealed in a food-grade plastic bag to prevent it from drying out.

USING FLORAL WIRES

Floral wires support and strengthen individual petals and leaves and make them easier to assemble into flowers and arrangements. The gauge you need depends on the size of the petal or leaf you want to make: the higher the gauge number, the finer the wire.

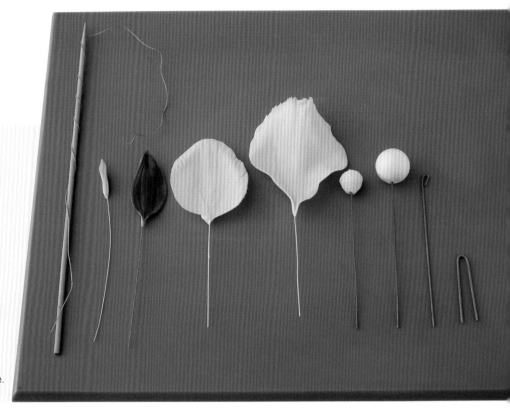

Common Wires and Their Uses

32-gauge green wire: Vines. Coil a 32-gauge wire around a bamboo skewer or the handle of a paintbrush to curl it.

30- to 26-gauge green wire: Leaves

30- to 26-gauge white wire: Petals

24- to 20-gauge hooked wire: Flower centres or bases. Hook the end of the wire with pliers so that it does not fall out of the base.

20- to 18-gauge wire: U-shaped pins. Cut a wire 5–6cm (2–2½") long and bend it into a 'U' shape with pliers. U-shaped pins are useful for fixing bouquets neatly to a cake.

Preparing Floral Wires

Keep floral wires straight when in storage, as warped wires are not suitable for sugar flowers or leaves.

1 I recommend cutting wires in half for most petals and leaves. Cut them into thirds for small petals and leaves, e.g. rose leaves. When adding to a stem for strength, use a whole wire or cut it in half depending on the length of the stem. Hold the wire at two points, one between your first and second finger and the other between your third finger and thumb, then cut between the two points with wire cutters or pliers. For thinner wires, align several wires and cut them together (A).

2 It is helpful to have a hook at the end of a wire when securing it into buds and flower centres. To create a hook at the end of the cut wires, use pliers to bend the very tip of the wire (B) then pinch the folded wire together to close the gap (C, D). Align several wires to create lots of hooks at once and save time.

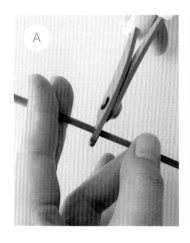

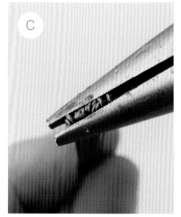

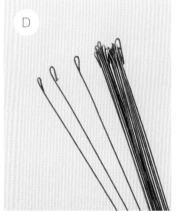

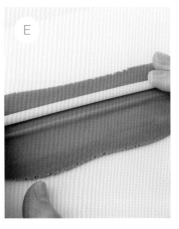

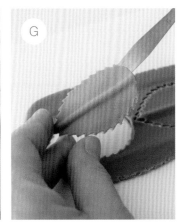
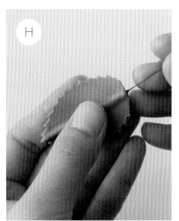

Small Wired Petals and Leaves

The most efficient way to make several small petals and leaves at the same time is to roll out a long strip of paste, leaving a ridge down the centre for the wire in each petal or leaf. Using the ridge as a guide, you can cut several petals or leaves from the paste.

1 Roll out a long strip of SFP. Place a CelStick widthways in the centre of the strip and thinly roll out the paste to the edge. Repeat on the other side, leaving a narrow vertical ridge for a wire along the centre of the paste (E). Cut out several petals/leaves along the strip, ensuring the ridge runs down the centre of each one (F, G).

2 Dip a floral wire into edible glue and gently insert it into the ridge of the petal or leaf: while doing so, press on either side of the central ridge with your thumb and forefinger to prevent the wire from sticking out of the paste (H).

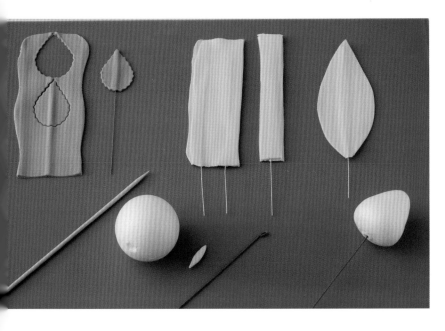

Large Wired Petals and Leaves

The most efficient way to make large wired petals and leaves is to sandwich two thin pieces of SFP together with the wire in between them.

1 Roll out two pieces of SFP into thin sheets approximately the same size. Line up some glued wires on one sheet of paste and lay the second sheet on top. Rub the SFP with your fingers to secure the wires between the two layers.

2 Cut the SFP into strips so that each strip of paste has a wire in the centre. Use a CelStick to thinly roll out the paste around the wire. Use a petal cutter or a template to cut out a petal or leaf.

Long Wired Leaves

This method is especially useful for long leaves as the single sheet of paste is lighter than the double layer needed for the large wired petals and leaves method above. Follow the instructions for dahlia leaves on page 98 or tulip leaves on page 144. It is best to hide the backs of the leaves when you arrange them as the wire may be visible beneath the paste.

Polystyrene Flower Base

Polystyrene shapes are my recommended base for sugar flowers. They are lighter than sugarpaste and they make sure that the central shape is precise.

1 Use a bamboo skewer to make a hole in the bottom of a polystyrene flower base. Brush a small amount of edible glue in the hole. Plug the hole with a small piece of SFP.

2 Make a small hook in the end of a wire and brush it with edible glue. Insert the wire into the SFP and leave it standing upright in a polystyrene block to dry.

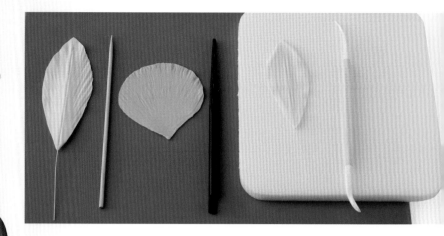

VEINING PETALS AND LEAVES

There are several different tools available for recreating the natural veins found in petals and leaves. Each produces a slightly different result.

Bamboo Skewer

Use for: narrow or teardrop-shaped petals, e.g. tulips and lilies

Place the petal on a non-stick board and use the bamboo skewer to emboss a central vein by laying it down the centre of the petal and pressing it into the paste. Slowly roll the tool across the surface of the paste, keeping the tip of the skewer pointing towards the base of the petal.

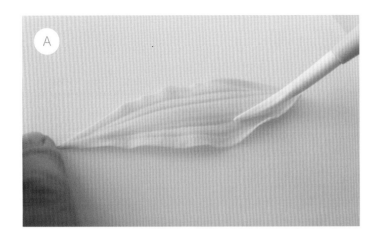

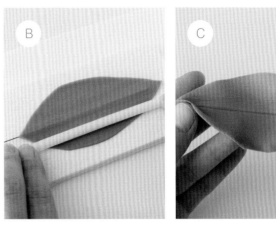

Veining Tool

Use for: petals with complex or reticulate veins, e.g. roses

Use the same method as for the bamboo skewer.

Leaf Shaping Tool

Use for: petals and leaves with simple veins, e.g. dahlia petals and peony leaves

Place the petal or leaf with the back facing upwards on a food-grade foam pad. Using a leaf shaping tool, mark lines along the length of the petal to create raised marks on the opposite side (A). Make sure that the tip of the leaf shaping tool is held at an angle against the paste, otherwise you may cut through it. Mark lines on the front of the petal or leaf if you need indented lines on the inside, such as for lily and peony leaves.

Moulded Veiners

Use for: leaves with more complex veins, e.g. roses, dahlias and tulips

When using a single veiner, place the leaf on top of the veiner with the front of the leaf facing down. Check it is correctly aligned and apply pressure to mark the veins.

When using a double veiner, lay the half of the veiner which has a groove along the central vein on the work surface. Place the leaf on top with the back facing down and the wired ridge in the groove of the veiner. Lay the other half of the veiner, which should have a raised ridge along the central vein, on top of the leaf and press it down firmly to create clear markings. Avoid pressing along the central wired vein as the wire may pierce the paste.

Corn Husk Textured Mat

Use for: leaves with close vertical veins, e.g. tulips

Place a leaf on the textured mat with the front of the leaf facing down. Roll out the paste from either side of the wire to the edges of the leaf using a CelStick (B). Lift the leaf from the mat and pinch down the central wired vein to secure it and give the leaf shape (C).

SHAPING PETALS AND LEAVES

To make your flowers look as natural as possible, it is important to smooth out and thin the very edges of each leaf or petal, even if the shape as a whole is supposed to be quite thick. To soften the edges of petals and leaves, place them on a foam pad. Run the tool of your choice over the very edge of the paste, so that the tool is half on the paste and half on the foam pad.

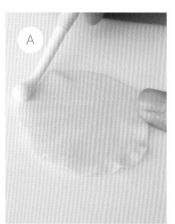
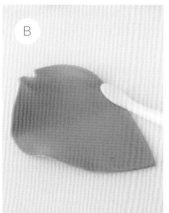
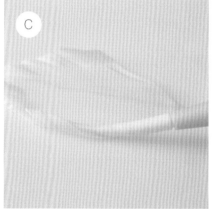
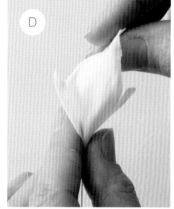

Frilled or Wavy Edges

Use a bone tool to frill the edge of a petal (A), or choose a flower shaping tool for making gentle waves (B).

Curved Edges

To curve the edges of a petal, place the petal on a foam pad. Run a leaf shaping tool, at an angle, from the edge of the petal down towards the base (C). Curve and shape the petal or leaf with your fingers (D).

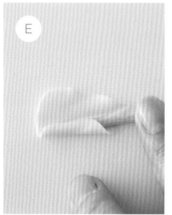
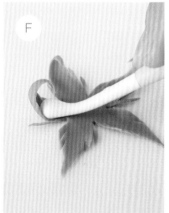

Always remember that your fingers are the best tools for making beautiful sugar flowers. When attaching a petal to a flower, make sure the previous petal is semi-dry and use your fingers to give it some finishing touches.

Curled Edges

To curl the edges of a single petal, place the petal on a foam pad and wrap the edges around a bamboo skewer (E). To curl the edges of a flower shape with multiple petals, such as a daisy, use a bone tool to stretch each petal outwards towards the tip, then bring the tool back inwards towards the centre (F).

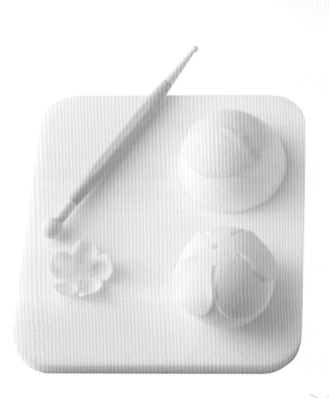

Cupped Petals

There are a few methods for cupping petals, depending on what you are making. For single petals, place the petal on a foam pad and cup the centre by gently pushing a ball tool into it in a circular motion. Alternatively, place a petal over a polystyrene ball former and cup the petal to fit the ball by pinching together excess paste at the centre of the base. For a small blossom shape, place the petal on a foam pad and push a small ball tool into the centre, holding it vertically.

Closed Petal Bases

To close the base of a petal, pinch it with flat nose tweezers or pliers after shaping (G–J). I recommend using plastic tools as metal ones may damage petals; pinch very gently if using metal tweezers or pliers.

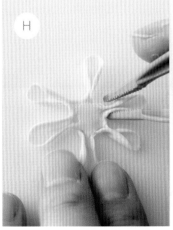

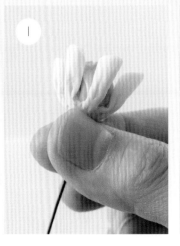

COLOURING PETALS AND LEAVES

The many different food colours available make it easy to create realistic sugar flowers.

Paste Food Colours

Paste food colours are the best to use for colouring SFP. Use a cocktail stick to pick up a tiny amount of the paste food colour and touch it on the SFP. Knead the colour into the paste until it has an even, consistent shade throughout. Avoid adding too much paste food colour to SFP as the paste will become sticky and the flower may not keep its shape. Instead, give petals and leaves a deeper colour by brushing them with dust food colours once they have been cut out and shaped.

Dust Food Colours

Use dust food colours to achieve natural shading on sugar flowers. Mix your chosen dust food colours in a paint palette with a soft brush, blot any excess colour from the brush onto kitchen paper and dust over the petal or leaf (A). I recommended using a cosmetic brush used exclusively for cake decorating for dusting whole petals or leaves as it holds a lot more colour than a paintbrush and has lots of fine hairs so the petal will be have a finer, deeper colour. If you are dusting the edge of a petal, use a flat paintbrush

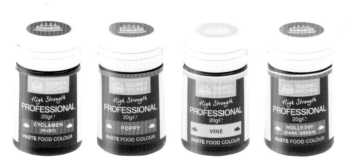

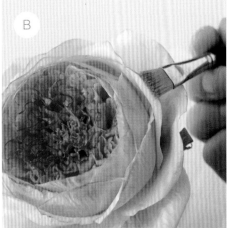

held at a right angle to the edge (B). Use white dust food colour to lighten previously dusted areas of petals or leaves (C).

Tip Make sure to dust petals or leaves before the flower paste dries out as this will help the colours to remain in place.

Edible Paints

For painting colour onto petals and leaves, I recommend using dust food colour mixed with a drop of clear alcohol, e.g. gin or vodka. Paint the petals or leaves with a fine paintbrush (D). It is also possible to use paste food colours for painting, however the colour may spread to another part of the petal or leaf because it takes longer to dry. If you need to remove some painted colour, gently rub a clean cotton bud moistened with clear alcohol over the spot.

Steaming

If you are using darker dust food colours then it is good idea to pass the dusted petals or leaves through the steam of a kettle to set the colour (E). However, you should only do this two or three times for each petal or leaf as too much steam can make dust colours look unnatural.

Glazing

To give leaves a shiny finish, paint confectioners' glaze over their surface with a paintbrush after steaming them. Alternatively, dip the leaves into the glaze then shake off the excess. If you would like to create a less shiny finish, make the confectioners' glaze thinner by mixing it with clear alcohol before use. It can be helpful to store confectioners' glaze in a clean, new, food-grade bottle similar to those used for nail polish as the dedicated brush inside the bottle is helpful for painting glaze over smaller leaves (F).

KEEPING THE SHAPE OF PETALS AND LEAVES

It is important to support sugar flowers while they dry so that they retain their shape.

Flower Stand

Flower stands are specifically made to support wired sugar flowers while they are drying. Use the holes to hang wired petals and small flowers upside down until they hold their shape.

Tissue Paper/Kitchen Paper

Tear a piece of tissue paper or kitchen paper into strips and bend each piece round to make a ring. Place the petal inside the ring so that the paper supports it in a gentle cupped shape.

Aluminium Foil

Cut a square of thin aluminium foil, make a cut from the edge to the centre of the foil and wrap the foil around the flower to prevent the petals from opening. Thread the wire of the flower into the hole of a flower stand vertically to keep the shape.

Polystyrene Block

If you are using a thick wire (24-gauge or below), push the end into a block of polystyrene once the flower centre is dry enough to hold its shape. Completed flowers can be stored in this way.

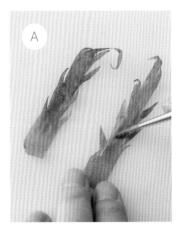

FLORAL TAPE CALYCES AND LEAVES

Floral tape can be used as an alternative to SFP when making a thin calyx or a leaf that would break easily if made from paste. Using floral tape for the leaves is a good idea when there are many thin leaves on a stem or when the flowers will be arranged close together.

1 Fold full-width green floral tape into several layers then cut the folds to make uniform lengths of tape.

2 Hold the lengths of tape together and use fine scissors to cut one end to a point. If making sepals for a calyx, make diagonal cuts into either side of the tape lengths, leaving 2cm (¾") uncut at the base.

3 Separate the lengths and stretch out each one. Twist the pointed ends and curl the tips between your thumb and finger.

4 Brush the outside of the tape with dust food colour. Brush the inside with edible glue (A) and attach the sepals to the flower (B) then tape the bottom 2cm (¾") to the wire at the base of the flower (C).

TAPING SUGAR FLOWERS AND ATTACHING SPRAYS

Floral tape is used to cover the wires of sugar flowers to form the stems and to secure one or more stems together.

Taping a Single Stem

1 Stretch the tape to release the glue. Place the tape around the wire, just below the flower head or the base of the leaf.

2 Holding the wire of the stem in one hand, squeeze the tape and the wire together with the fingers of your other hand. Twist the stem firmly so the tape is attached to the wire.

3 Continue to tape down the wire, pulling the tape diagonally downwards and making it as taut as possible.

4 To make a thicker stem, wrap thin strips of kitchen paper around the wire before taping it as above.

Securing Flowers to a Cake with a Posy Pick

Hold the flowers against the cake to arrange them and decide on the position. Use a cocktail stick to mark where to insert a posy pick in the cake, setting it beneath the upper part of the stem of the bouquet. Put the bouquet to one side and insert a posy pick filled with sugarpaste into the cake. Place a U-shaped pin (see page 18) around the stem and insert the two ends of the pin into the posy pick to secure the bouquet on the cake.

Tip

You can always use a dummy cake for any tier with a large spray. This makes the cake lighter and avoids damaging the real cake. You can arrange the spray on the dummy well in advance.

Securing Flowers to a Cake with Sugarpaste

Make a ball of sugarpaste and secure it to the cake or board with edible glue. Push the wires from the flowers into the sugarpaste. You can usually fix a small spray or a large flower onto the cake using this method, which is useful for attaching flowers where you cannot insert a posy pick.

IMPORTANT NOTE

Never push wires directly into a cake or covering that is to be eaten and always remove any wired flowers, posy picks and other inedible items safely before the cake is cut.

Rose

With its sweet fragrance and outstanding beauty, the rose has been beloved around the world for thousands of years, playing a significant part in cultures as far back as ancient Egypt. There are so many types of lovely roses in different colours that for me it is the 'Queen of Flowers' when it comes to decorating cakes. Make the petals very thin for a more natural look.

Rose Foundations

POLYSTYRENE FLOWER CENTRE

Option A: Polystyrene Cone Flower Base

1 Wire a polystyrene cone flower base using the guide on page 19. Use a 2.4cm (1") polystyrene cone and a 22-gauge floral wire, unless specified otherwise in the project.

2 Thinly roll out some SFP and cut out a petal using the no. 3 cutter from SK Multi-Flower Cutter Set 1. Use the curved edge of cutter no. 4 to cut off the curved edge of the petal about 2cm (¾") from the tip of the curve. Slightly widen the remaining part of the petal by rolling it out with a CelStick. Smooth the cut edges with a flower shaping tool.

3 Brush edible glue over the pointed tip of the cone. With the curved edge of the petal facing upwards, place the point of the wired cone in the centre of the petal, slightly below the edge of the paste. Wrap the petal around the cone centre, one side at a time (A).

4 Cut out two petals with the no. 2 cutter from SK Multi-Flower Cutter Set 1 and frill the edges with a bone tool. Glue them evenly spaced around the flower centre, slightly higher than the previous petal (B).

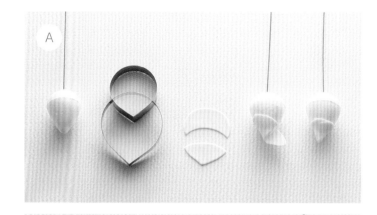

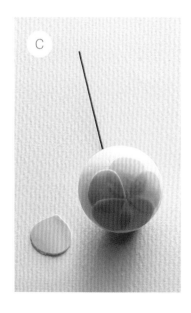

Option B: Polystyrene Ball Bud Base

1 Flatten the top of a polystyrene ball flower base slightly with sandpaper. Wire it using the polystyrene flower base guide on page 19. Use a 3cm (1⅛") polystyrene ball and a 22-gauge floral wire, unless specified otherwise in the project.

2 Thinly roll out some SFP and cut out five petals using cutter no. 1 from SK Multi-Flower Cutter Set 1. Smooth the edges with a flower shaping tool.

3 Glue the petals to the top of the polystyrene ball one by one, evenly spaced, with the points at the centre. Tuck the edge of the last petal under the first petal (C).

4 Brush the petals with dust food colour.

D

COTTON THREAD FLOWER CENTRE

Option A: Cotton Thread Stamen Centre (Without Pistil)

1 Wind cotton thread around your index and middle fingers 20–30 times. Cut the thread from the reel and remove it from your fingers. Twist the thread once in the middle to make a figure of eight then fold one ring over the other.

2 Pass one end of a 30-gauge wire through the ring of thread, fold the wire in half over the cotton then twist the wires together twice to hold it in place. Wind the shorter end of the wire twice around the base of the cotton ring, then twist the wires together down the length to make them into one.

3 Cut through the cotton loop to make individual stamens then trim them to approximately 1cm (³/₈") long. Dip the ends into edible glue and then into pollen dust food colour.

4 Tape the wired stamens to a hooked floral wire to make a stem (D). Use a 20-gauge green wire unless otherwise specified in the project.

Option B: Cotton Thread Stamen and SFP Pistil Centre

1 Bend a 30-gauge green wire in half then twist the wire together at the bend to make a small loop.

2 Wind cotton thread around your index, middle and ring fingers approximately 50 times. Cut the thread from the reel and remove it from your fingers. Twist the thread once in the middle to make a figure of eight then fold one ring over the other.

3 Pass one end of the wire through the ring and twist the wires twice beneath the thread to hold it in place, leaving the small loop in the wire made in step 1. Wind the shorter end of the wire twice around the base of the cotton ring, then twist the wires together down the length to make them into one (E).

4 Cut through the cotton loop to make individual stamens (F) then trim them to approximately 2cm (¾") long. Dip the threads in edible glue until completely covered (G). Once the glue has dried a little, splay out the threads and curl them using a cocktail stick or a bamboo skewer (H, steps continued overleaf).

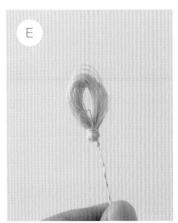

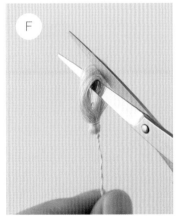

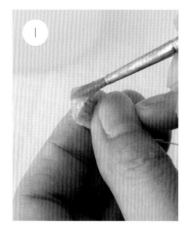

5 Hold the cotton stamens together, brush edible glue on the tips of the threads then dip them into pollen dust food colour (I, J).

6 Roll a small ball of SFP. Insert a cocktail stick into the centre of the paste, brush the ball with a little edible glue then brush it with pollen dust food colour. Insert another cocktail stick into the side of the flower centre to pick it up and attach it to the small loop of wire at the centre of the thread (K, L).

7 Tape the wired stamens to a hooked 20-gauge green floral wire to make a stem.

ENGLISH ROSE FLOWER CENTRE

1 Make a cotton thread stamen centre (without pistil) using the basic method on page 31.

2 Cut a 4cm (1½") polystyrene ball in half and put one half aside. Cut off the top of the remaining dome to flatten it, then smooth the edges with sandpaper. Make a hole in the centre of the dome with a bamboo skewer, making sure the skewer goes all the way through the ball vertically.

3 Brush the domed side of the polystyrene flower base with edible glue. Roll out 30g (1oz) of sugarpaste in the same colour as chosen for the petals and use it to cover the domed side of the polystyrene. Re-insert the bamboo skewer so the hole is visible (M).

4 Turn the flower base over so the flat side is facing upwards. Cut out a circle of sugarpaste using a 4cm (1½") circle cutter and attach it to the flat side using edible glue. Re-insert the bamboo skewer so the hole is visible.

5 Fill the hole on the domed side of the flower base with SFP. Insert the wire stem of the cotton thread stamen centre into the hole at the flat side of the flower base and secure with edible glue at the base of the thread (N). Leave to dry.

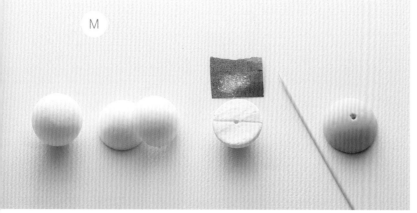

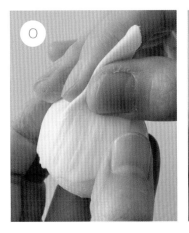
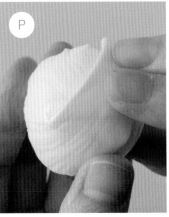
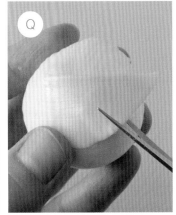
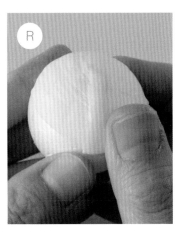

CUPPED PETALS

Non-wired Cupped Petals

1 Thinly roll out some SFP and cut out the petal with a rose petal cutter. Vein it using a veining tool and soften the edges with a bone tool.

2 Brush the veined side of the petal with dust food colour.

3 Place the petal over the top of a polystyrene ball former. Fit the petal to the former from top to bottom and pull together both sides of the excess paste from the bottom centre of the petal (O).

4 Fold the excess paste to one side and cut it away with fine scissors (P, Q). Smooth the cut edges with your finger (R). Leave the petal to semi-dry on the former.

Tip Make a ball former for drying cupped petals in the right shape by cutting off the base of a polystyrene ball to stop it from rolling.

Wired Cupped Petals

1 Cut out a wired rose petal using the guide for large wired petals and leaves on page 19 and a 28-gauge wire.

2 Vein both sides of the petal with a veining tool and frill the edges with a bone tool. Brush both sides of the petal with dust food colour.

3 Place the petal over the top of a polystyrene ball former without bending the wire. Pinch together the excess paste under the wire at the base of the petal with your thumb and index finger (S).

4 Lift the petal off the former and cut out the triangle of excess paste between the base of the petal and the wire (T).

5 Return the petal to the former. Overlap the cut ends of the petal (U) then bend the wire down to cover the join in the paste. Press with your thumbs to ensure the petal is snug against the former (V).

6 Remove the excess paste from around the wire and pinch the edges of the petal to shape it outwards (W). Tape the petal to the flower.

CALYX

Option A: Flower Paste Calyx

1 Roll out some Pale Green SFP, keeping it fairly thick. Cut out the paste with a calyx cutter. Stretch out the sepals with a bone tool and make cuts up the edges of each one with fine scissors. To curl the sepals, draw the bone tool from the tips to the centre (X).

2 Turn the calyx over, insert the wire of the rose into the centre, thread the calyx up the wire and attach its sepals to the base of the rose with edible glue.

3 Make a small ball of Pale Green SFP and attach it under the calyx.

4 Brush the calyx with Holly/Ivy and Vine dust food colours and add a touch of Cyclamen to the edges.

 Tip You can also use the Mexican hat technique on page 17 to make a flower paste calyx. I have specified this technique for a couple of the flowers which need a smaller ball below the calyx.

Option B: Floral Tape Calyx

1 Make calyces using floral tape following the guide on page 27. Fold the green floral tape into five 8cm (3¹⁄₈") long layers.

2 Brush the outside of the tape with Holly/Ivy and Vine dust food colours and add a touch of Cyclamen to the edges (Y).

3 Attach each calyx sepal to the base of the flower with edible glue (Z). Bring together the ends of each calyx with floral tape and wrap it down the wire to secure them in place (AA).

 Tip I use floral tape to make calyces for flowers with cupped petals such as the English rose because they are more fragile.

LEAVES

1 Cut out a wired rose leaf using the guide for large wired petals and leaves on page 19, Pale Green SFP, a cutter from the Orchard Products

Rose Leaf Cutter Set of 4 (R576A) and a 28- or 30-gauge green wire. For each set of three you will need one larger and two smaller leaves. Alternatively, you could make five leaves per stem. Vein the leaves with a veiner from the set of three SK Great Impressions Rose Leaf Veiners and leave them to dry.

2 Tape the wires of each leaf individually then tape the two smaller leaves on either side and slightly below the large leaf.

3 Dust with Holly/Ivy and Leaf Green dust food colours and add touches of Cyclamen to the edges. Steam the leaves and leave them to dry.

4 Coat the leaves with confectioners' glaze using your preferred method if you would like to give it a shiny finish (AB).

AB

STEM AND ASSEMBLY

1 Roses have multiple leaves for every flower. Tape the leaf stem approximately 2cm (¾") under the base of the leaves alternately down the flower stem. Dust Cyclamen dust food colour around the joins in the stems.

2 If you would like to add more leaves to the flower, make a closed bud using the method in step 1 for the hybrid tea rose buds on page 41. Add a hooked 20-gauge green wire to the bud stem and tape them together to make a long stem using green floral tape. Tape the leaves to the bud stem in the same way as for the flower stem above.

3 Tape the bud stem to the middle of the flower stem, arranging the bud to sit slightly higher than the flower.

Hybrid Tea Rose

The hybrid tea rose is said to be the first modern rose. With a long, upright stem, it is a popular cut flower and accounts for the majority of roses sold by florists. Hybrid tea roses have large blooms with a pointed form and come in a huge range of colours. In my experience, all sugar florists enjoy reproducing this beautiful flower.

EDIBLES

SK Sugar Florist Paste (SFP): Candy Pink and Pale Green

SK Professional Dust Food Colours: Cyclamen, Holly/Ivy, Poinsettia and Vine

SK Designer Bridal Satin Dust Food Colour: White Satin

SK Designer Moon Beam Lustre Dust Food Colour: Ruby

EQUIPMENT

2.8cm (1¹/₈") polystyrene cone

20- and 22-gauge green floral wires

SK Multi-Flower Cutter Set 1: nos. 2, 4, 5 and 7

SK Great Impressions Tea Rose Petal Veiner: Very Large (7cm/2¾")

Green floral tape

Orchard Products Rose Calyx Cutter: R11C (7cm/2¾")

Orchard Products Rose Leaf Cutter Set of 4: R576A (2cm, 2.5cm, 3.5cm and 4cm/³/₄", 1", 1³/₈" and 1¹/₂")

SK Great Impressions Rose Leaf Veiner Set of 3: Small, Medium and Large (3cm, 3.7cm and 4.5cm/1¼", 1½" and 1¾")

ESSENTIAL EDIBLES AND EQUIPMENT (SEE PAGE 10)

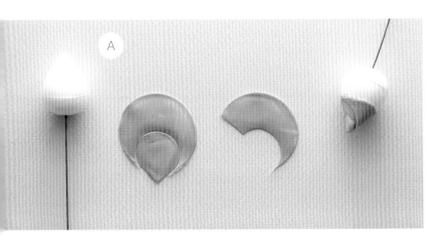

FLOWER CENTRE

Wire a 2.8cm (1¹/₈") polystyrene cone with a 20-gauge green wire using the guide on page 19.

PETALS

Inner Petals

1 Thinly roll out some Candy Pink SFP and cut out a petal with the no. 5 petal cutter from SK Multi-Flower Cutter Set 1. Cut out the inside of the petal using the no. 2 petal cutter with the pointed ends aligned to make a crescent shaped petal. Cut the point from one end of the crescent. Brush edible glue over the tip of the wired polystyrene cone. Place the blunt end of the crescent on the rose base, with the inner curve slightly higher than the tip, and wrap the petal around it (A).

2 Thinly roll out some SFP and cut out two petals with a no. 4 petal cutter. Vein them using a veining tool and soften the edges with a bone tool.

3 Brush the veined inside of the petals with a mixture of Poinsettia and Cyclamen dust food colours. Brush the outside of the petals with a mixture of White Satin and Ruby Moon Beam dust food colours.

4 Glue the two petals around and slightly higher than the central petal, overlapping alternate edges.

5 Make six petals as in steps 2–3 using the no. 5 petal cutter. Attach them so they are overlapping and slightly higher than the previous petals (B).

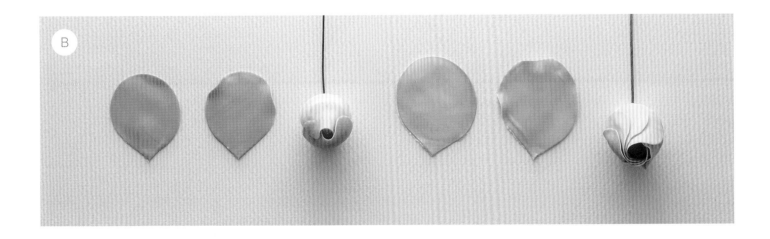

Outer Non-wired Petals

1 Thinly roll out some Candy Pink SFP and cut out three petals with a no. 7 cutter from SK Multi-Flower Cutter Set 1. Vein them using a veining tool and soften the edges with a bone tool. Curl the edge of each petal outwards with a bamboo skewer and use a ball tool to cup the petals.

2 Brush the veined inside of the petals with a mixture of Poinsettia and Cyclamen dust food colours (C). Brush the outside of the petals with a mixture of White Satin and Ruby Moon Beam dust food colours.

3 Brush a little edible glue on the point of each petal and attach them, evenly spaced, around the previous petals. Open the petals slightly with your fingers.

4 Gather any excess paste from each petal at the stem of the flower and cut it away with fine scissors (D).

5 Make five petals as in steps 1–2. Attach the petals at the base of the flower around the previous layer of petals, with the centre of each petal overlapping a gap between the previous ones. If you would like to make a smaller, 9cm (3½") tea rose, the petals are complete at this stage so you can skip the following instructions for outer wired petals.

Outer Wired Petals

1 To create a larger, 12.5cm (5") tea rose the additional layers of petals should be wired. Cut out a wired rose petal using the guide for large wired petals and leaves on page 19, a 28-gauge wire and the no. 7 cutter from SK Multi-Flower Cutter Set 1. Cut a 5mm (¼") deep 'V' of paste from the base of the petal using a cutting wheel.

2 Vein both sides of the petal with a veining tool or tea rose petal veiner and frill the edge with a bone tool. Curl the edge of each petal outwards with a bamboo skewer and use a ball tool to cup the petals.

3 Dust the petals as in step 2 for the outer non-wired petals (E).

4 Repeat steps 1–3 to make three more wired petals then arrange them, evenly spaced, around the flower and secure with floral tape.

5 If you would like to make the flower bigger still, make four petals with the no. 7 cutter following steps 1–2 for the outer non-wired petals. Glue the petals in between the outer two layers of petals.

CALYX AND LEAVES

Make and attach the calyx using the foundation method for a flower paste rose calyx on page 34, Pale Green SFP and a 7cm (2¾") calyx cutter. Make the leaves following the method for rose leaves on the same page.

BUDS

1 For a fully closed bud, make a rose base by rolling a 2cm (¾") cone of Candy Pink SFP then insert a glued, hooked 20-gauge wire (F). Leave the base to dry overnight. Make a calyx and use it to cover the rose base from the bottom upwards.

2 For an opening bud, make the first stages of a full rose using a wired polystyrene cone base and steps 1–5 for the inner petals. Make a calyx and use it to cover the petals from the bottom upwards.

3 For a more open bud, make the first stages of a full rose using a wired polystyrene cone base, steps 1–5 for the inner petals and steps 1–4 for the outer non-wired petals. Make a calyx and attach it so that the sepals cover the joins of the rose petals.

ASSEMBLY

Tape a set of rose leaves below each flower and bud, leaving a gap on the stem beneath the flower head to show it off. Tape the bud stem below the leaves on the flower stem, positioning the bud slightly higher than the flower.

Old Garden Rose

There are many different types of old garden rose, also known as heritage roses, which were bred before the creation of the hybrid tea rose in 1867. I believe that you cannot help but love this charming flower, which has a deep cupped form with many petals.

●───────────────── ● ● ● ● ─────────────────●

EDIBLES

SK Sugar Florist Paste (SFP):
Pale Green and White

SK Designer Pollen Dust Food Colours:
Apple Green and Dark Golden

SK Professional Dust Food Colours: Cyclamen,
Holly/Ivy and Vine

SK Designer Bridal Satin Dust Food Colour:
White Satin

EQUIPMENT

Orchard Products Five Petal Cutters: F5 and F6B
(5cm and 9cm/2" and 3½")

PME Supatube Piping Nozzle: no. 5

Beige cotton thread

20-, 22- and 30-gauge green floral wires

28-gauge white floral wires

Green floral tape

4cm, 5cm and 6cm (1½", 2" and 2⅜") polystyrene
ball formers

SK Multi-Flower Cutter Set 1: nos. 2, 3, 4 and 6

Orchard Products Rose Calyx Cutter: R11C
(7cm/2¾")

Orchard Products Rose Leaf Cutter Set of 4: R576A
(2cm, 2.5cm, 3.5cm and 4cm/¾", 1", 1⅜" and 1½")

SK Great Impressions Rose Leaf Veiner
Set of 3: Small, Medium and Large
(3cm, 3.7cm and 4.5cm/1¼", 1½" and 1¾")

2.4cm (1") polystyrene cone

ESSENTIAL EDIBLES AND EQUIPMENT (SEE PAGE 10)

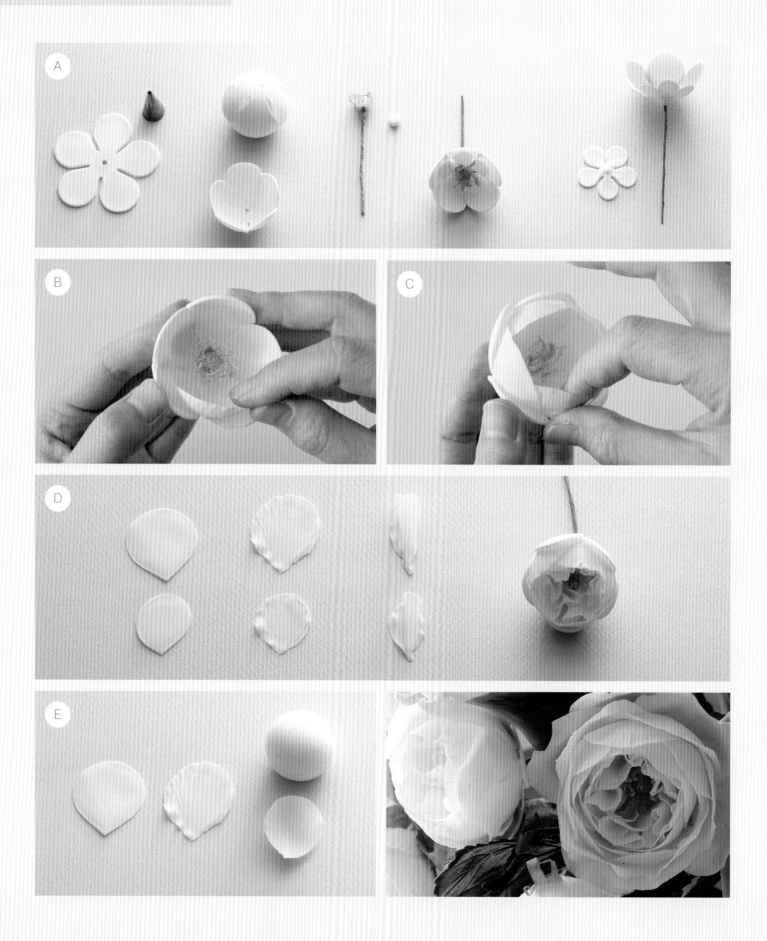

FLOWER CENTRE

1 Roll out some White SFP and cut out a flower shape with the 9cm (3½") five petal cutter. Cut a hole in the centre of the flower shape using the tip of a no. 5 piping nozzle.

2 Lightly dust a 5cm (2") polystyrene ball former with icing sugar or cornflour, place the flower shape over the former and gently press it around the ball to cup the petals. Leave it to semi-dry.

3 Meanwhile, make the centre using the foundation method for a cotton thread stamen and SFP pistil centre on page 31 with beige cotton thread and Dark Golden pollen dust food colour. Use Pale Green SFP and Apple Green pollen dust food colour for the pistil.

4 Before the paste is completely dry, remove the flower shape from the ball former. Position the petals to slightly overlap and fix each petal to the next with edible glue. Leave the petals to dry completely.

5 Glue a small ball of White SFP on the central hole inside the dry flower shape. Brush the base of the cotton thread centre with edible glue and thread the wire down through the hole in the flower shape to secure it in the ball of paste.

6 Press a flattened ball of White SFP against the hole in a foam pad to make a cone at the centre. Remove the paste from the foam pad and place it on a non-stick board, with the cone facing upwards. Use a CelStick to roll the paste out from the centre, then cut out a flower shape with the 5cm (2") five petal cutter.

7 Thread the wire of the flower centre through the middle of the flower shape and out through the cone. Attach the flat side of the shape underneath the flower centre with edible glue (A).

8 Leave the flower centre standing upright in a flower stand to dry completely.

PETALS

Inner Petals

1 Make five petals using the foundation method for non-wired cupped rose petals on page 33, White SFP, the no. 6 cutter and a 4cm (1½") ball former.

2 Brush the veined side of the petals with White Satin dust food colour then add a little Vine dust food colour at the base of each petal.

3 Attach the petals inside the flower centre using edible glue, with the centre of each petal covering a join in the cupped flower shape base (B, C).

4 Thinly roll out some White SFP and cut out five petals using the no. 4 cutter. Vein the petals with a veining tool and frill the edges with a bone tool. Dust the petals as in step 2. Gather the paste together at the base of the petal to make it narrower. Place each petal on a 4cm (1½") ball former, veined side down, to set.

5 Glue the petals in front of and in between the previous layer of petals, with the veined side facing the centre of the flower (D).

6 Repeat steps 4–5 to make and attach five more petals using the no. 3 petal cutter. If necessary, adjust the number of petals to suit the amount of space in the flower centre.

Outer Petals

1 Make five petals using the foundation method for non-wired cupped rose petals on page 31, White SFP, the no. 4 cutter and a 4cm (1½") ball former (E).

2 Brush the outside of the petals with White Satin dust food colour then add a little Vine dust food colour at the base of each petal.

3 Attach the petals one by one behind the flower shape with edible glue so they are evenly spaced and at the same height as the inner petals.

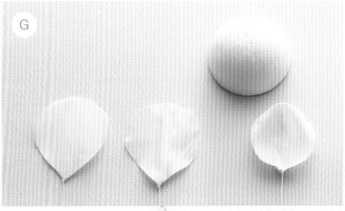

4 Repeat steps 1–3 to make five petals using the no. 6 cutter and a 5cm (2") ball former, attaching them slightly lower than the previous petals.

5 Repeat step 4 to make and attach a layer of five petals using the no. 6 cutter and a 6cm (2³⁄₈") ball former (F).

6 Make five petals using the foundation method for wired cupped rose petals on page 33, the no. 6 cutter, 28-gauge white wires and a 6cm (2³⁄₈") ball former. Dust the petals as in step 2 (G).

7 Use floral tape to attach the petals evenly spaced around the base of the previous petals then tape down the wire (H).

CALYX

Make the calyx using the foundation method for a flower paste rose calyx on page 34, Pale Green SFP and a 7cm (2¾") calyx cutter. Or, if you prefer, make a floral tape rose calyx using the foundation method on page 34.

H

BUDS

1 Make the bud base using the foundation method for a polystyrene cone rose flower base on page 30, a 2.4cm (1") polystyrene cone, 22-gauge wire and White SFP.

2 Thinly roll out some White SFP and cut out five petals using the no. 4 petal cutter. Vein the petals with a veining tool and soften the edges with a bone tool. Dust the petals as in step 2 for the inner petals.

3 Attach the petals evenly spaced and close around the bud base with edible glue, sitting slightly higher than the central petal.

4 Make and attach a calyx in the same way as for the flower then tape down the wire of the bud (I).

LEAVES, STEM AND ASSEMBLY

Make the leaves and stem and assemble the flower following the foundation methods on pages 34–35.

English Rose

WITH SIMPLE INNER PETALS

Also known as Austin roses, English roses are the creation of David Austin, a well-known rose breeder from England. These roses have characteristics of both old garden roses and modern varieties. I'm grateful to him for introducing hundreds of rose cultivars over the past 60 years.

EDIBLES

SK Designer Pollen Dust Food Colour:
Pale Golden

SK Fairtrade Sugarpaste: Ballerina Pink

SK Sugar Florist Paste (SFP):
Pale Pink and White

SK Professional Dust Food Colours: Cyclamen,
Holly/Ivy, Rose and Vine

SK Designer Bridal Satin Dust Food Colour: White
Satin

SK Quality Food Colour (QFC) Dust: Pink

EQUIPMENT

Yellow cotton thread

3cm and 4cm (1⅛" and 1½") polystyrene balls

5cm and 6cm (2" and 2⅜") polystyrene
ball formers

20-, 22- and 30-gauge green floral wires

28-gauge white floral wires

Green floral tape

4cm (1½") circle cutter

Orchard Products Carnation Cutters:
2.5cm, 3.3cm and 4cm (1", 1¼" and 1½")

SK Multi-Flower Cutter Set 1: nos. 1, 4, 5,
6 and 7

Orchard Products Rose Leaf Cutter Set of 4: R576A
(2cm, 2.5cm, 3.5cm and 4cm/¾", 1", 1⅜" and 1½")

SK Great Impressions Rose Leaf Veiner
Set of 3: Small, Medium and Large
(3cm, 3.7cm and 4.5cm/1¼", 1½" and 1¾")

ESSENTIAL EDIBLES AND EQUIPMENT (SEE PAGE 10)

FLOWER CENTRE AND BASE

Make the centre using the foundation method for an English rose flower centre on page 32. Roll a very small amount of Ballerina Pink sugarpaste into a sausage and wrap it around the base of the cotton thread flower centre, on top of the covered polystyrene base.

PETALS

Inner Petals

1 Roll out some Pale Pink SFP and cut out two flower shapes with the 2.5cm (1") carnation cutter. Stretch the paste by running a bone tool from the centre of the circle to the edge of each frond. Vein with a veining tool.

2 Cut each flower shape into quarters to make eight petals. Glue four of the petals around the ring of sugarpaste so they are evenly spaced at the base of the cotton thread centre. Glue the remaining four petals in between the previous petals.

3 Repeat steps 1–2 to create two sets of petals using the 3.3cm (1¼") carnation cutter and attach them around the smaller petals (A).

4 Roll a small amount of Ballerina Pink sugarpaste into a sausage and wrap it around the base of the petals. Smooth the paste with your fingers to make the flower base more spherical, with a dome shape under the attached petals (B).

5 Repeat steps 1–2 to create two sets of petals using the 4cm (1½") carnation cutter and attach them around the previous petals (C).

6 Brush the central petals with Rose dust food colour mixed with a small amount of Cyclamen.

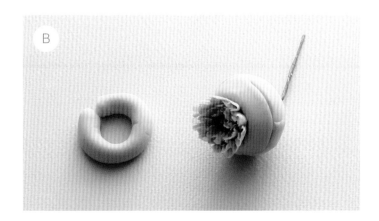

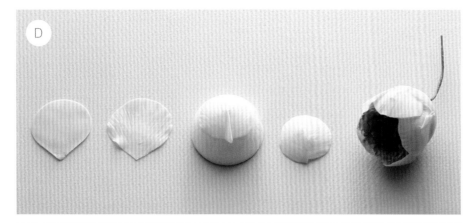

Outer Petals

1 Knead a small amount of White SFP into some Pale Pink SFP to make a paler pink paste for the outer petals.

2 Make five petals using the foundation method for non-wired cupped rose petals on page 33, the no. 4 cutter from SK Multi-Flower Cutter Set 1 and a 5cm (2") polystyrene ball former. Dust the veined side of the petals with White Satin dust food colour then brush a little Vine at the base of each petal.

3 Use edible glue to attach the five petals so they are evenly spaced around the inner petals, with the top edge of the petals slightly higher than the centre (D).

4 Repeat step 2 to make five petals using the no. 6 cutter and a 5cm (2") ball former. Attach the petals around the previous layer using edible glue, with the centre of each petal covering a join in the previous layer.

5 Repeat step 4 to make five petals using the no. 6 petal cutter and a 6cm (2³/₈") ball former (E).

6 For the fourth layer, repeat step 4 to make five petals using the no. 7 cutter and a 6cm (2³/₈") ball former. Attach these petals at the bottom of the flower base with edible glue (F).

7 Make the final five petals using the foundation method for wired cupped rose petals on page 33, the no. 7 cutter, 28-gauge white wires and a 6cm (2³/₈") ball former (G). Use floral tape to attach the petals at the base so they are evenly spaced around the previous petals. Tape down the wire.

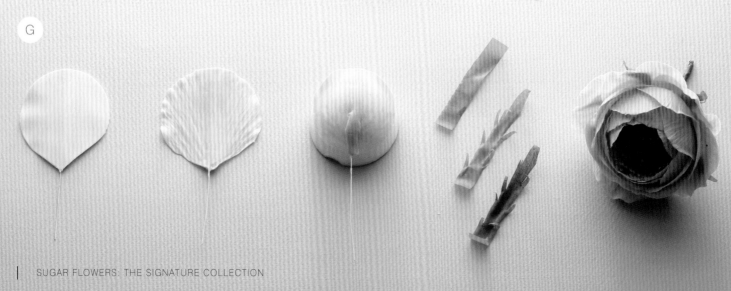

CALYX

Make and attach the calyx using the foundation method for a floral tape rose calyx on page 34.

BUD

1 Make the bud base using the foundation method for a polystyrene ball rose bud base on page 30.

2 Follow steps 1–3 for the inner petals of the flower to cut out and shape one set of each size of petals. Attach them close together around the bud centre in a flatter, closed position (H).

3 Brush the petals with White Satin dust food colour and catch the tips of the petals with a mixture of Rose and Cyclamen.

4 Make the outer petals for the bud following steps 1–2 for the outer petals of the flower; you will need three petals made with both of the nos. 5 and 6 petal cutters.

5 Brush the veined side of the petals with White Satin dust food colour then add a little Pink dust food colour at the base of each petal.

6 Attach the three smaller petals with edible glue so they are evenly spaced and high enough up the flower base to curve around the edge of the inner petals. Attach the three larger petals around the base of the bud.

7 Make and attach the calyx as for the flower then tape down the wire of the bud (I).

LEAVES, STEM AND ASSEMBLY

Make the leaves and stem and assemble the flower following the foundation methods on pages 34–35.

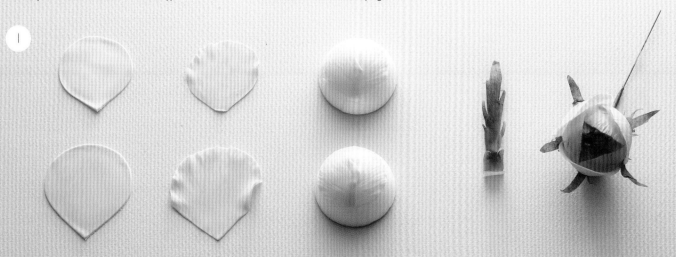

English Rose

WITH COMPLEX INNER PETALS

This rose has very impressive inner petals. If you make the flower paste for the inner petals very thin and don't arrange them too uniformly, they will have a more natural look.

EDIBLES

SK Designer Pollen Dust Food Colour:
Pale Golden

SK Fairtrade Sugarpaste: Ballerina Pink

SK Sugar Florist Paste (SFP): Cream,
Pale Green and Pale Pink

SK Professional Dust Food Colours:
Cyclamen, Holly/Ivy and Vine

SK Designer Bridal Satin Dust Food Colour:
White Satin

SK Quality Food Colour (QFC) Dust: Pink

EQUIPMENT

Yellow cotton thread

3cm and 4cm (1$\frac{1}{8}$" and 1$\frac{1}{2}$") polystyrene balls

5cm and 6cm (2" and 2$\frac{3}{8}$") polystyrene
ball formers

20-, 22- and 30-gauge green floral wires

28-gauge white floral wires

Green floral tape

4cm (1$\frac{1}{2}$") circle cutter

SK Multi-Flower Cutter Set 1: nos. 1–7

Orchard Products Rose Calyx Cutter: R11C
(7cm/2$\frac{3}{4}$")

Orchard Products Rose Leaf Cutter Set of 4:
R576A (2cm, 2.5cm, 3.5cm and 4cm/$\frac{3}{4}$", 1",
1$\frac{3}{8}$" and 1$\frac{1}{2}$")

SK Great Impressions Rose Leaf Veiner
Set of 3: Small, Medium and Large
(3cm, 3.7cm and 4.5cm/1$\frac{1}{4}$", 1$\frac{1}{2}$" and 1$\frac{3}{4}$")

ESSENTIAL EDIBLES AND EQUIPMENT (SEE PAGE 10)

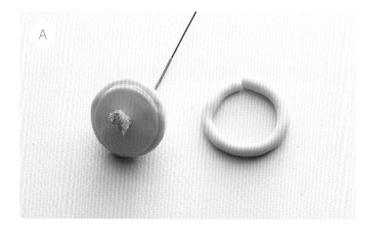

FLOWER CENTRE

Make the centre using the foundation method for an English rose flower centre on page 32.

PETALS

Inner Petals

1 Roll a small amount of Ballerina Pink sugarpaste into a sausage, shape it into a ring and attach it to the rim of the flat surface of the flower base with edible glue (A).

2 Knead together Pale Pink and Cream SFP to make a very pale pink paste for the petals.

3 Thinly roll out some paste and cut out two petals with each of the nos. 1, 2 and 3 petal cutters from SK Multi-Flower Cutter Set 1. Frill the edges of the six petals with a bone tool (B).

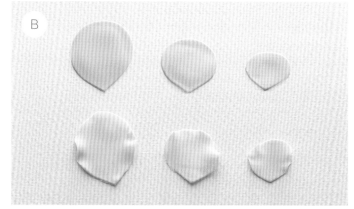

4 Place the petals in a pile in order of size with the largest two petals at the bottom, securing them all together at the base of the petals with a little edible glue. Pinch the bunch of petals from the back with your thumb and index finger then cut away the excess paste at the back to make it a flat surface (C). Repeat to make five more bunches of petals.

5 Attach three evenly spaced bunches of petals around the cotton thread flower centre with edible glue. Adjust the pointed base of each petal bunch to ensure it is against the flower centre and lightly open the petals so the back petal rests on the ring of the flower base. Attach the remaining three bunches in between the previous bunches and adjust in the same way (D).

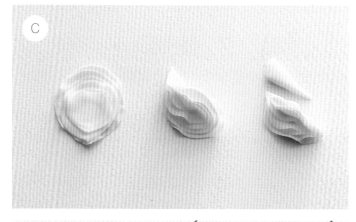

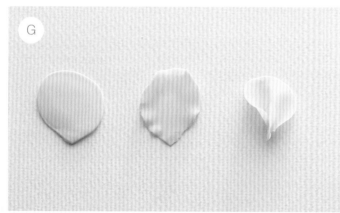

6 Dust the petals with White Satin dust food colour and add a touch of Pink at the centre of each bunch.

Outer Petals

1 Make seven petals using the foundation method for non-wired cupped rose petals on page 33, the no. 5 cutter and a 5cm (2") ball former, but vein both sides of the petals (E). Dust the petals with White Satin dust food colour.

2 Attach the petals so they are evenly spaced around and at the same height as the inner petals whilst the inner petals are still soft.

3 Repeat step 1 to make seven petals using the no. 6 cutter and a 6cm (2³⁄₈") ball former (F). Attach the petals evenly spaced around and slightly lower than the previous layer, with the centre of each petal covering a join in the previous petals.

4 If you find some gaps between the inner and outer petals, make a few additional petals as in step 1 using the no. 3 cutter then pinch the pointed base of each petal (G). Brush a little glue in the gap on the flower and attach the petal using a flower shaping tool.

5 Repeat step 3 to make and attach a layer of five petals using the no. 7 cutter and a 6cm (2³⁄₈") ball former (H).

6 Make five petals using the foundation method for wired cupped rose petals on page 33, the no. 7 cutter, 28-gauge white floral wire and a 6cm (2³⁄₈") ball former (I). Dust the petals with White Satin dust food colour. Use floral tape to attach the petals evenly spaced around the base of the previous petals then tape down the wire (J, K).

CALYX

Make the calyx using the flower paste rose calyx foundation method on page 34, Pale Green SFP and a 7cm (2¾") calyx cutter. Or, if you prefer, make a floral tape rose calyx using the foundation method on page 34.

BUDS

1 Make the bud base with a 3cm (1¹/₈") polystyrene ball and 22-gauge green floral wire using the foundation method for a polystyrene ball rose bud base on page 30.

2 Thinly roll out some paste and cut out five petals with each of the nos. 2 and 4 petal cutters. Vein the outside of the petal with a veining tool and frill the edges with a bone tool. Dust the veined side of the petals with White Satin and Pink dust food colours.

3 Attach the smaller five petals so they are evenly spaced and close around the bud base with edible glue. Wrap the larger petals around the bud so they are interlocking and slightly higher than the previous layer, with the centre of each petal covering a join in the previous layer.

4 Make and attach a calyx in the same way as for the flower then tape down the wire of the bud (L).

LEAVES, STEM AND ASSEMBLY

Make the leaves and stem and assemble the flower following the foundation methods on pages 34–35.

Wild Rose

Also known as species roses, wild roses will lend a natural look to your sugar flower arrangements. This single-flowered rose comes in shades of pink and white; I have opted for a pale cream to emphasise the simple beauty of this variety.

EDIBLES

SK Designer Pollen Dust Food Colours:
Apple Green and Pale Golden

SK Sugar Florist Paste (SFP): Cream
and Pale Green

SK Professional Dust Food Colours:
Cyclamen, Daffodil, Edelweiss, Holly/Ivy
and Vine

EQUIPMENT

Pale yellow cotton thread

20-, 22- and 30-gauge green floral wires

28-gauge white floral wires

Green floral tape

SK Multi-Flower Cutter Set 1: nos. 2, 3, 4, and 7

Orchard Products Rose Calyx Cutter: R11C
(7cm/2¾")

Orchard Products Rose Leaf Cutter Set of 4:
R576A (2cm, 2.5cm, 3.5cm and 4cm/¾", 1",
1³/₈" and 1½")

SK Great Impressions Rose Leaf Veiner
Set of 3: Small, Medium and Large
(3cm, 3.7cm and 4.5cm/1¼", 1½" and 1¾")

2.4cm (1") polystyrene cone

ESSENTIAL EDIBLES AND EQUIPMENT (SEE PAGE 10)

FLOWER

1 Make the centre using the foundation method for a cotton thread stamen and SFP pistil rose centre on page 31. Use pale yellow cotton thread and Dark Golden pollen dust food colour for the stamens, and use Pale Green SFP and Apple Green pollen dust food colour for the pistil.

2 Cut out a wired petal from Cream SFP using the no. 4 petal cutter and the foundation method for large wired petals and leaves on page 19. Use the pointed end of the no. 7 petal cutter to cut away a small triangle at the top edge of the petal. Stretch the petal slightly on both sides using a CelStick to make it heart shaped.

3 Soften the edge of the petal with a flower shaping tool to give it a gentle wave. Pinch the base of the petal into the wire then bend the wire inside the petal to curve it inwards slightly. Gently curl the top edges back with your fingers.

4 Brush the middle of the petal with a mixture of Daffodil and Edelweiss dust food colours, then dust Vine at the base of the petal.

5 Make eight petals in total following steps 2–4.

6 Use floral tape to attach three petals evenly spaced around the base of the flower centre. Tape the remaining five petals evenly spaced around the inner petals then tape down the wire (A).

CALYX

1 Use the Mexican hat foundation technique on page 17 to cut out a calyx from Pale Green SFP with the 7cm (2¾") calyx cutter. Smooth the calyx with a flower shaping tool.

2 Place the rounded end of a CelStick in the centre of the flat side of the calyx and gently push down into the mound to make it hollow. Brush a little edible glue in the hollow, insert the wire of the flower and thread the calyx up to the base of the flower. Secure the calyx sepals to the flower with a little more glue.

3 Dust the calyx and the floral tape just below it with Holly/Ivy and Vine dust food colours, then add a little Cyclamen at the edges of the calyx sepals (B).

BUD

1 Make the bud base using the foundation method for a polystyrene cone rose bud base on page 30, a 2.4cm (1") polystyrene cone, 22-gauge green wire and Cream SFP.

2 Thinly roll out some Cream SFP and cut out three petals using the no. 3 petal cutter. Soften the edges with a bone tool. Attach the petals to the bud with edible glue so that they are overlapping and close to the base. Brush the base of the petals with Vine dust food colour.

3 Cut out three more petals with the no. 4 petal cutter, soften the edges with a bone tool then curl them using a bamboo skewer. Dust the base of the petals with Vine dust food colour on both sides. Glue the petals to the bud so the centre of each petal covers a join in the previous layer, then open them up slightly.

4 Make the calyx using the foundation method for a flower paste rose calyx on page 34, Pale Green SFP and a 7cm (2¾") calyx cutter. Tape down the wire of the bud (C). To make a closed bud, follow step 1 of the instructions for a hybrid tea rose bud on page 41.

LEAVES AND ASSEMBLY

Make the leaves following the foundation method for rose leaves on pages 34–35. To assemble the arrangement, place the wild rose flowers in the centre and tape the buds, rose leaves and spray roses around them. Tape them down the stem of the wild rose so they don't hide the flower head.

Spray Rose

Unlike the other roses in this chapter, spray roses have several flowers per branch: short individual stems on a single large stem. You have the choice to arrange the spray roses all in one piece or as separate stems. You will also be able to add some curves to your sugar flower arrangement as I have included some vines.

● ● ● ● ●

EDIBLES

SK Designer Pollen Dust Food Colour: Russet

SK Sugar Florist Paste (SFP): Cream, Pale Green and White

SK Professional Dust Food Colours: Cyclamen, Holly/Ivy, Leaf Green and Vine

SK Quality Food Colour (QFC) Dust: Pink

EQUIPMENT

Pale yellow cotton thread

22-, 26-, 28-, 30- gauge green floral wires

Green floral tape

Orchard Products Five Petal Cutters: F7, F6A and F5 (3.5cm, 4.2cm and 5cm/ 1³/₈", 2⁵/₈" and 2")

Orchard Products Calyx Cutter: R12 (3.6cm/1³/₈")

1.5cm (⁵/₈") polystyrene balls

FMM Rose Leaf Cutter: 2.5cm (1")

SK Great Impressions Rose Leaf Veiner Set of 3: Small, Medium and Large (3cm, 3.7cm and 4.5cm/1¼", 1½" and 1¾")

ESSENTIAL EDIBLES AND EQUIPMENT (SEE PAGE 10)

FLOWER

1 Make the flower centre using the foundation method for a cotton thread rose stamen centre (without pistil) on page 31. Use pale yellow cotton thread and Russet pollen dust food colour for the stamens. Tape the stamens to a 26-gauge hooked floral wire.

2 Knead together some White and Cream SFP to make a pale cream paste.

3 Use the Mexican hat technique to cut out a flower shape using the 3.5cm (1³/₈") five petal cutter.

4 Soften the edges with a flower shaping tool and cup the petals using a ball tool. Brush the base of the petals with Vine dust food colour and the edges with a little Pink.

5 Insert the wire of the flower centre into the centre of the flower shape. Use edible glue to attach it, arranging the petals so they overlap closely around the stamens (A). Leave it to dry.

6 Thinly roll out some pale cream SFP and cut out a flower shape using the 4.5cm (2³/₄") five petal cutter. Shape and colour the petals as in step 4. Thread the wire of the flower through the centre of the shape and attach it at the base of the previous petals with edible glue. Overlap the petals.

7 Repeat step 6 to make and attach another layer of petals using the 5cm (2") five petal cutter. Open out the outer petals slightly with your fingers (B). Hang the flower upside down on a flower stand to dry.

CALYX

Make the calyx using the foundation method for a flower paste rose calyx on page 34, Pale Green SFP and a 3.6cm (1³/₈") calyx cutter. Tape down the wire of the flower (C).

BUDS

Opening Bud

1 Make a bud base using the foundation method for a polystyrene ball rose bud base on page 30, a 1.5cm (⁵/₈") polystyrene ball, 28-gauge wire and pale cream SFP. Instead of a single petal cutter, use the 3.5cm (1³/₈") five petal cutter then separate the shape into five individual petals by rolling a cutting wheel out from the centre. Once attached, brush the petals with a little Vine dust food colour and catch the edges with Pink (D).

2 Thinly roll out some paste and cut out a flower shape with the 4.2cm (2⁵/₈") five petal cutter. Shape and colour the petals as in step 4 for the flower. Thread the flower shape up the wire and attach it with edible glue (E).

3 Use the Mexican hat foundation technique on page 17 to cut out a calyx from Pale Green SFP with the 3.6cm (1³/₈") calyx cutter. Smooth the calyx with a flower shaping tool.

4 Place the rounded end of a CelStick into the centre of the flat side of the calyx and gently push down into the mound to make it hollow. Brush a little edible glue in the hollow, insert the wire of the flower and thread the calyx up to the base of the bud. Secure the calyx sepals to the petals with a little more glue.

5 Colour the calyx in the same way as the flower calyx (F).

Closed Bud

1 Make a 1.5cm (⁵/₈") long, thin teardrop shape with Pale Green SFP. Insert a glued, hooked 28-gauge green wire into the base and leave it dry.

2 Make a calyx using the same method as for the flower. Attach the calyx to cover the bud base and pinch the top to give it a pointed shape (G).

LEAVES

1 Make five wired rose leaves using the foundation technique for small wired petals and leaves on page 19, Pale Green SFP, the 2.5cm (1") rose leaf cutter and 30-gauge green wire. Vein them with a rose leaf veiner then leave them to dry.

2 Tape the wires of each leaf individually then tape two leaves on either side and slightly below a single leaf. Repeat to add another pair of leaves.

3 Brush the leaves with Holly/Ivy and Leaf Green dust food colour and add touches of Cyclamen to the edges. Steam the leaves and leave them to dry (H).

4 Coat the leaves with confectioners' glaze using your preferred method if you would like to create a sheen.

ASSEMBLY

1 Tape a closed and an opening bud together, setting the opening bud slightly below the closed bud. Add a 22-gauge wire to the stem as you tape down to make it longer and thicker Tape a flower slightly below the buds (I).

2 Finally, add a stem of rose leaves with the taping point approximately 6cm (2³/₈") below the base of the closed bud (J, K).

3 Make five bunches of spray roses and tape them together to make a rose cluster.

Lily

This graceful flower appears in stories from many different ancient cultures. In Greek mythology the lily is a symbol of Hera, the goddess of marriage and family. The secret to making a sugar lily is to overlap the petals neatly and they will make an elegant cake decoration.

Lily Foundations

FLOWER CENTRE

Pistil

1 Roll a small sausage of White SFP. Brush a small amount of edible glue onto a white floral wire; use a 26-gauge white wire when making the style for the pistil and 28-gauge white wires when making filaments for the stamens, unless specified otherwise in the project. Insert the wire through the length of the sausage (A).

2 Place the sausage on a non-stick board and roll and stretch the paste down the wire until it is long and thin, allowing the wire to protrude from one end of the style (B).

3 Flatten the paste lightly with a cake smoother (C). Cut away the excess paste from either side using a cutting wheel (D).

4 Smooth the surface of the style between your fingers and thumb. Lightly curve the upper part of the style (E). Leave it to dry.

5 Roll a small ball of SFP for the stigma. Use small scissors to mark three lines in the ball that meet in the centre at the top and bottom (F).

6 Attach the base of the ball to the top of the style with edible glue and leave it to dry.

7 Brush the stigma with the specified dust food colour.

Stamens

1 Repeat steps 1–4 of the pistil to make the stamen filaments, using 28-gauge white wires and making them slightly shorter than the style. You will need six stamens for each flower.

2 Roll some SFP into a 2cm (¾") long sausage to make the anther for each stamen. Taper it at both ends with your thumb and forefinger.

3 Make a well in the centre of the sausage with a flower shaping tool. Gently pinch the paste from behind the well with your thumb and forefinger to bring the two sides together (G).

4 Glue the anther to the top of a filament with the indented side facing out and the filament curving into the back of the anther (H). Leave the stamen to dry.

5 Brush the anther with the specified dust food colour.

Assembly

1 Thinly roll out some White SFP. Cut out a rectangle of paste to the size specified in the project, brush it with edible glue and wrap it around the base of the pistil (I).

2 Brush the belt of paste with edible glue and attach the bases of the stamens around it, making sure the anthers are all level and below the stigma (J, K). Wrap the base of the flower centre in kitchen foil to hold it together until dry then remove the foil.

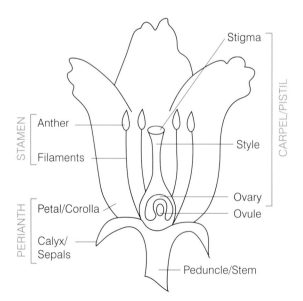

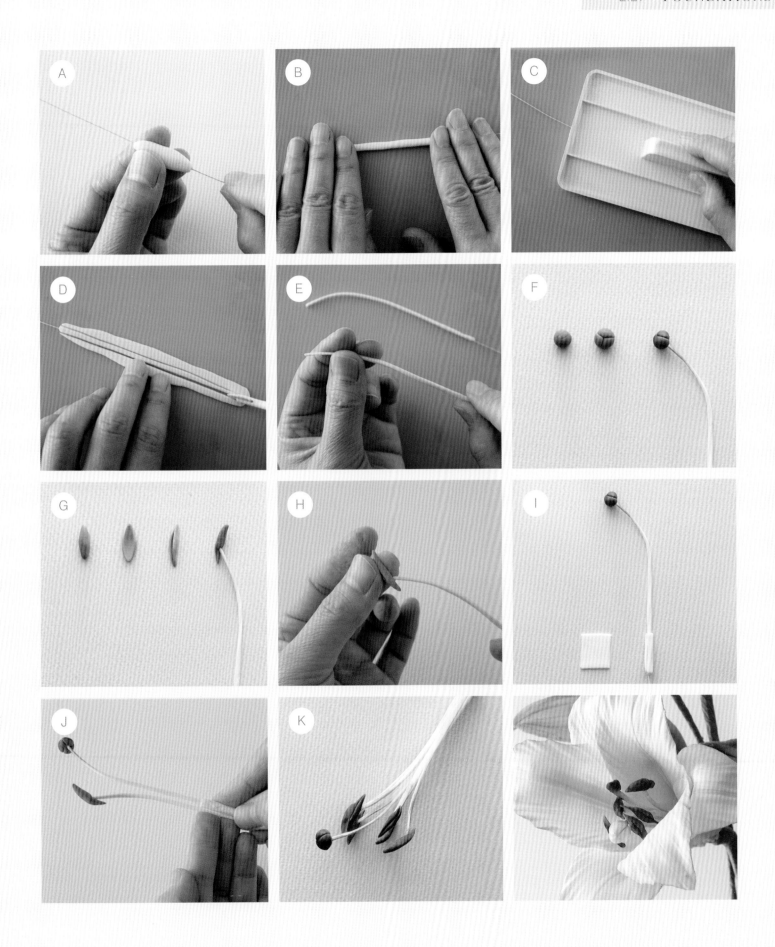

PETALS

1 Cut out three wired petals using the large wired petals and leaves guide on page 19 and the specified cutter.

2 Mark three lines down the centre of each petal by pressing down on the paste with a bamboo skewer, one along the central vein and one on either side.

3 Vein the petals by rolling a bamboo skewer along the edges, keeping the tip of the tool pointing towards the base of the petal (L). Alternatively, you could use a specifically-designed petal veiner.

4 Brush the petals with the dust food colours specified in the project.

5 Gently bend the wire inside the petals to shape them. Curve the lower part of the petal up towards the centre whilst moving the thumb and finger of your other hand up and down the wire to gently curve it backwards. Bend the top of the petal backwards and pinch the tip to curl it under (M).

6 Brush a little edible glue at the base of the flower centre then secure the petals evenly around it with green floral tape. The petals should overlap at the base.

7 Wrap tissue paper around the base of the petals and leave the flower to dry upright until it is firm, so it maintains its shape. A bottle or a vase with a narrow neck can be useful for providing support.

8 Make three outer petals in the same way as the inner petals. Arrange and tape them to overlap the spaces between the inner petals, with the petal bases fitting tightly together. Tape down the wire then leave the flower to dry upright.

BUD

1 Make a teardrop shape with the same colour of SFP as the flower. Bend a hook in the end of a 22-gauge green wire, brush it with edible glue and insert it into the base of the teardrop (N). Leave it to dry.

2 Roll a piece of SFP into a long sausage with tapered ends. Use a CelStick to roll out the shape from the centre on both sides, leaving a 1cm (³/₈") long, thin cylinder of paste at the base.

3 Place the specified cutter above the cylinder and gently mark the petal shape without cutting through (O). Remove the cutter and follow the lines to cut out the petal with a cutting wheel, leaving the cylinder in place (P).

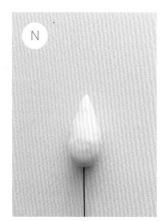

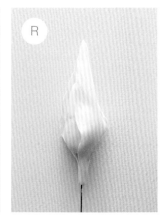

4 Vein the petal as in step 3 of the petals for the main flower and dust them in the colour specified in the project (Q). Make three petals in total.

5 Brush the wired teardrop and the 1cm (³/₈") of wire beneath it with edible glue. Hold the cylinder of paste at the base of the first petal against the glued section of wire first, then wrap the petal around the teardrop. Attach the remaining petals in the same way so they overlap each other then shape them with your fingers at the top to hide the teardrop (R).

STEM

Wrap thin strips of kitchen paper around the wire then wrap green floral tape around them to make a thicker stem.

LEAF

1 Knead together some White and Holly/Ivy SFP until evenly mixed.

2 Roll out and wire some of the mixed green SFP for the leaves using the large wired petals and leaves guide on page 19 and a 28-gauge wire. Use cutter nos. 6 and 7 from the SK Multi-Flower Cutter Set 3 with the most

pointed end at the top to mark the leaf shape without cutting through the paste. Cut out the leaf shape with a cutting wheel, leaving 1cm (³/₈") of wired paste at the top of the stem.

3 Place the leaf on a foam pad and use a flower shaping tool to smooth and soften the surface, working from the outside into the centre. Mark a central vein with a bamboo skewer and draw two parallel lines on either side with a leaf shaping tool (S).

4 Bend the wire so the top part of the leaf curves back. Curve the bottom 1cm (³/₈") of the edges up with your thumb and forefinger and pinch the top.

5 Brush the leaf with a mixture of Holly/Ivy and Leaf Green dust food colours then pass it through steam to set the colour (T). To create a sheen, dip the leaf in confectioners' glaze.

ASSEMBLY

Tape the leaf to the stem of a lily flower or bud, fitting the hollow at the bottom 1cm (³/₈") of the leaf around the stem.

Maiden Lily

The delicate pink, alpine *Lilium rubellum* is called maiden lily or 'otome-yuri' in Japan. Its elegant, trumpet-shaped form is similar to the Easter lily (*Lilium longiflorum*), another native Japanese flower.

EDIBLES

SK Sugar Florist Paste (SFP): Holly/Ivy, Pale Pink, Soft Peach and White

SK Designer Bridal Satin Dust Food Colour: White Satin

SK Professional Dust Food Colours: Cyclamen, Holly/Ivy, Leaf Green, Nasturtium and Vine

SK Quality Food Colour (QFC) Dust: Pink

EQUIPMENT

SK Multi-Flower Cutter Set 3: nos. 6, 7, 8 and 9

26- and 28- gauge white floral wires

22- and 28-gauge green floral wires

Green floral tape

ESSENTIAL EDIBLES AND EQUIPMENT (SEE PAGE 10)

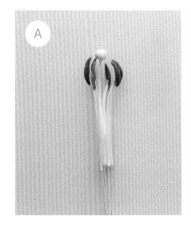

FLOWER CENTRE

1 Make the flower centre using the foundation method on page 74 (A). The style for the pistil should be 8cm (3¹/₈") long and the filaments for the six stamens should be 6cm (2³/₈") long. Just make a subtle curve at the upper part of these filaments. Use White SFP for the stigma and Soft Peach SFP for the anthers.

2 Dust the style and filaments with White Satin dust food colour. Brush the top of the style and the bases of the filaments with Vine. Brush the stigma with Vine dust food colour then paint it with confectioners' glaze to give it a shiny finish. Brush the anthers with a mixture of Cyclamen and Nasturtium dust food colours. The rectangular belt of paste used to attach the stamens to the pistil should measure 4cm x 1cm (1¹/₂" x ³/₈").

PETALS

1 Knead together some Pale Pink and White SFP to create a very light pink colour.

2 Make and attach three inner petals using steps 1–8 of the foundation method on page 76, 26-gauge white wires and the no. 9 cutter (B). Dust the surface of the petals with White Satin dust food colour. Add a little Pink dust

food colour to the edges of the petals and Vine to the base. Attach the petals so they form a bell shape around the centre (C).

3 Repeat step 2 to make three outer petals using the no. 8 cutter, this time making them slightly less curved (D). Use green tape to attach the outer petals to the flower, positioning them between the previous petals and making sure they hug the inner petals tightly. Tape down the wire then leave the flower to dry upright supported by tissue paper.

BUD

Make the bud using the foundation method on pages 76–77. Start with a 4cm (1½") long teardrop shape of very light pink SFP and use the no. 6 cutter with the most pointed end at the top. Dust the bud petals lightly with White Satin dust food colour then brush a little Pink at the edges and Vine at the bases of the petals.

STEM, LEAF AND ASSEMBLY

Make the stem and a leaf and attach it using the foundation methods on page 77.

Casablanca Lily

With large, pure white petals and deep red stamens, *Lilium* 'Casa Blanca' is a classic oriental lily and one of the most popular species. To make *Lilium* 'Le Rêve' as seen on the wedding cake on page 193, simply brush pink dust food colour and paint dots on the petals of the Casablanca lily.

• • ● •

EDIBLES

SK Sugar Florist Paste (SFP): Cyclamen, Holly/Ivy, Poinsettia, Soft Peach and White

SK Designer Bridal Satin Dust Food Colour: White Satin

SK Professional Dust Food Colours: Cyclamen, Edelweiss, Holly/Ivy, Leaf Green, Nasturtium and Vine

EQUIPMENT

SK Multi-Flower Cutter Set 3: nos. 6 and 7

SK Casablanca Lily Petal Cutter Set of 2

26- and 28-gauge white floral wires

22- and 28-gauge green floral wire

Green floral tape

ESSENTIAL EDIBLES AND EQUIPMENT (SEE PAGE 10)

FLOWER CENTRE

1   Make the flower centre using the foundation method on page 74. The style for the pistil should be 12cm (4¾") long, and the filaments for the six stamens should be 9cm (3½") long. Use a combination of Poinsettia and Cyclamen SFP to make the stigma and Soft Peach SFP to make the anthers.

2   Dust the style and filaments with White Satin dust food colour, then brush the upper parts with Leaf Green dust food colour and the bases with Vine. Dust the stigma with Cyclamen and the anthers with Cyclamen and Nasturtium dust food colours. The rectangular belt of paste used to attach the stamens to the pistil should measure 2cm x 1cm (³/₄" x ³/₈").

PETALS

1   Cut out a wired inner petal using the large wired petals and leaves guide on page 19, White SFP, a 26-gauge white wire and the wider cutter from the SK Casablanca Lily Cutter Set of 2 (A).

2   Vein the petal using step 3 of the foundation method for lily petals on page 76. Turn the petal over, place it on a foam pad and use a ball tool to frill the edges (B). Use a leaf shaping tool to mark dots over the back of the petal approximately 1.5cm (⁵/₈") apart, working along the veined lines (C).

3   Use fine scissors to cut a shallow section from the base of the front of the petal and lift it up slightly to create a protruding point (D). Repeat to create points over the entire lower half of the petal.

4   Brush the surface of the petal with a mixture of Edelweiss and White Satin dust food colours, then brush Vine along the central vein and Leaf Green at the base of the petal.

5   Shape the petal using step 5 of the foundation method for lily petals on page 76.

6   Make two more petals in this way then follow steps 6–7 of the foundation method for lily petals on page 76 to attach the three inner petals to the flower centre (E). Leave the flower to set.

7   Cut out three wired petals as in step 1 above using the narrower cutter from the SK Casablanca Lily Cutter Set of 2 (F). Repeat steps 2–5 (above) to texture, dust and shape the petals. Use green floral tape to attach the petals to the flower over the gaps between the inner petals (G). Leave the flower to set upright, supporting it with tissue paper around the base of the petals.

BUDS

Make the bud using the foundation method for lily buds on pages 76–77, starting with a 5cm (2") long teardrop shape of White SFP and using the no. 7 petal cutter from SK Multi-Flower Cutter Set 3 with the most pointed end at the top. Dust the bud petals lightly with White Satin dust food colour and brush a little Vine at the base of the petals.

STEM AND LEAF

Make the stem and a leaf using the foundation methods on page 77.

ASSEMBLY

1   Strengthen the stem and make it thicker following the foundation method for a tulip stem on page 143. Bend the neck of the flowers and buds forwards slightly.

2   Since the Casablanca lily has large petals with a pointed end, assemble the flowers so the ends of the petals do not touch any other petals or buds. Tape a bud to a flower stem, setting it towards the back and facing away from the flower. Tape a leaf at the point where the stems join.

3   Tape another flower under the previous bloom, setting the tip of the highest petal in between the lower petals of the previous flower. Tape another bud to the same place on the stem, then tape three leaves around the point where the flower and bud join.

Chandelier Lily

Lilium ledebourii is a rare species of lily native to Azerbaijan and Iran. This flower's downward-facing blooms have given it the common name of chandelier lily. What a lovely creature!

EDIBLES

SK Sugar Florist Paste (SFP): Cyclamen, Pale Pink, Soft Peach and White

SK Designer Bridal Satin Dust Food Colour: White Satin

SK Professional Dust Food Colours: Cyclamen, Holly/Ivy, Nasturtium, Rose and Vine

EQUIPMENT

SK Multi-Flower Cutter Set 3: nos. 6 and 7

26- and 28-gauge white floral wires

22-gauge green floral wires

Green floral tape

ESSENTIAL EDIBLES AND EQUIPMENT (SEE PAGE 10)

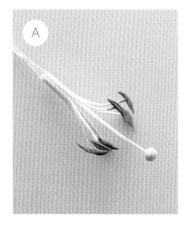
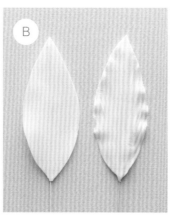
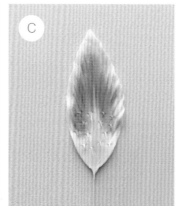
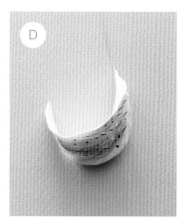

FLOWER CENTRE

1   Make the flower centre using the foundation method for a lily centre on page 74 (A). The style should be 9cm (3$\frac{1}{2}$") long and the filaments should be 6cm (2$\frac{3}{8}$") long. Use White SFP for the stigma and Soft Peach SFP for the anthers.

2   Dust the style and filaments with White Satin dust food colour then brush the upper and lower parts with Vine dust food colour. Brush the stigma with Vine dust food colour then paint it with confectioners' glaze to give it a shiny finish. Brush the anthers with a mixture of Cyclamen and Nasturtium dust food colours. The rectangular belt of paste used to attach the stamens to the pistil should be 2cm x 1cm ($\frac{3}{4}$" x $\frac{3}{8}$").

PETALS

1   Knead a small amount of White SFP into some Pale Pink SFP to create a very light pink colour.

2   Cut out and vein three inner petals using steps 1–3 of the foundation method for lily petals on page 76, 28-gauge white wires and the no. 7 cutter with the most pointed end at the top of the petal. Frill the edges of the petals using a ball tool (B).

3   Brush the surface of the petal lightly with White Satin dust food colour. Brush a mixture of Rose and Cyclamen dust food colours over the middle and upper parts of the petals, leaving the edges uncoloured. Brush Vine dust food colour at the base of the petal and continue it up the centre slightly (C).

4   Use fine scissors to cut a shallow section from the base of the front of the petal and lift it up slightly to create a protruding point. Repeat to create points over the entire lower half of the petal.

5   Mix a little clear alcohol into Cyclamen dust food colour to make a paint. Use a fine brush to paint the protruding points and add dots on the pink dusted areas.

6   Shape the petals following step 5 of the foundation method for lily petals on page 76. Draw the sides at the base of the petal together to curve it inwards and bend the petal backwards into a tight curve that is almost semi-circular (D).

7   Attach and leave the petals to set using steps 6–7 of the foundation method for lily petals on page 76.

8   Make three outer petals using step 8 of the foundation method, 26-gauge white wires and the no. 6 cutter, with the most pointed end at the top of the petal.

LEAVES

As there are many thin leaves on this stem it is best to make them with floral tape using the guide to floral tape calyces and leaves on page 27. Use the same shade of green floral tape as for the stem and fold it into layers approximately 8cm (3¹/₈") in length. Dust one side of each leaf with a mixture of Holly/Ivy and Vine dust food colours then catch the edges with Cyclamen.

STEM AND ASSEMBLY

Add a 22-gauge green wire to the bottom of the flower, wrap thin strips of kitchen paper around the wire then wrap green floral tape around it to make a thicker stem. Use pliers to bend the neck of the flower downwards as is characteristic of the chandelier lily. Tape the leaves to the stem in pairs with the dusted side facing upwards.

Dahlia

Dahlias have a punchy presence which dominates other flowers. They are part of the daisy family and can be divided into 14 or 15 groups based on the size and type of flower head, from tiny pompons to giant-flowered cactus dahlias.

There are many vivid colours for you to choose from to add impact to sugar flower arrangements. Although the 'petals' of a dahlia are technically known as ray florets, I have referred to them as petals in this chapter to keep sugar flower methods consistent throughout the book.

Dahlia Foundations

FLOWER CENTRE

Option A: Polystyrene Base

Use the polystyrene flower base guide on page 19, a 2cm (¾") polystyrene ball and a 20-gauge green floral wire to make the flower centre. Attach the central petals following the instructions below.

Option B: Flower Paste Base

Insert a hooked 20-gauge green floral wire into a 3g (<¹⁄₈oz) ball of Pale Green SFP. Leave it to dry completely before attaching the central petals.

Central Petals

1 Roll out some SFP and use the guide to cutting out petals and leaves on pages 16–17 to cut out a shape with a six petal flower cutter in the size specified in the project.

2 Place the flower shape on a foam pad. Draw a bone tool out from the centre and along each petal to stretch the paste (A).

3 Cut down the centre of each petal using fine scissors (B). Use a leaf shaping tool to curve the petals inwards, drawing the tool from the tip of each half petal to the centre of the flower shape (C).

4 Brush the prepared polystyrene or SFP flower centre with a little edible glue. Thread the flower shape up the wire then close the petals around the ball until it is completely covered (D, E).

PETALS

Flat Petals

1 Thinly roll out some SFP and cut out a petal, either wired or unwired as specified in the project, following the guide on page 19. Use the cutter and wire specified in the project.

2 Mark three lines at the centre of the petal, one along the central vein and one on either side: for an unwired petal use a leaf shaping tool or for a wired petal mark the lines by pressing down with a wooden skewer (F). This is the front of the petal.

3 Flip the petal over and place it on a foam pad. Soften the edges with a flower shaping tool. Use a leaf shaping tool to mark two lines on either side of the central lines (G).

4 Flip the petal over again. Pinch the base inwards and use your fingers to shape the top of the petal (H).

Rolled Petals

1 Make the petal following steps 1–3 of the foundation method above for flat dahlia petals without a wire.

2 Flip the petal over again and place it on a foam pad. Place a wooden skewer on one side with the skewer tip at the centre of the curved base of the petal. Wrap the petal edge over it (I). Roll the petal onto the skewer, stopping at the central line (J).

3 Lift the base of the other side of the petal and fix it to the centre using a small amount of edible glue (K). Remove the skewer. Pinch the top of the petal inwards (L).

BUD

Large Bud

1 Make the bud centre in the same way as the flower centre on page 94 using a 2.5cm (1") polystyrene ball and the same colour of SFP as the flower petals (M). When shaping the central petals in step 2, stretch them to give the flower shape a 7cm (2¾") diameter in order to cover the polystyrene base.

2 Roll out some SFP and cut out a shape using a 7cm (2¾") sunflower cutter. Cut the shape into quarters so each segment has five petals. Use a bone tool to stretch each petal from the base to the tip.

3 Widen each petal slightly using a CelStick then soften all of the edges with a flower shaping tool. Use a leaf shaping tool to mark a central vein on the inside of each petal (N).

4 Fold the petals in on themselves and pinch them together at the base of the segment. Repeat with the remaining three petal segments then attach them around the flower centre at evenly spaced intervals with edible glue (O).

5 Repeat step 2 to make four more petal segments. Use a cutting wheel to separate each petal so there are 20 individual petals. Widen and soften the edges of the petals as in step 3. Use a leaf shaping tool to mark three lines on the inside of each petal.

6 Curl the top edge of each petal on either side using a wooden skewer. Pinch the base and the tip of each petal with your finger and thumb.

7 Attach the petals so they are evenly spaced around the previous layer using edible glue (P).

8 Dust the bud to match the flowers. To make an even larger bud, make and attach larger petals instead of steps 5–7.

Small Bud

1 Repeat steps 1–4 for the large bud but use a 2cm (¾") polystyrene ball for the base and do not stretch the petals so much.

2 Dust the small bud to match the flowers.

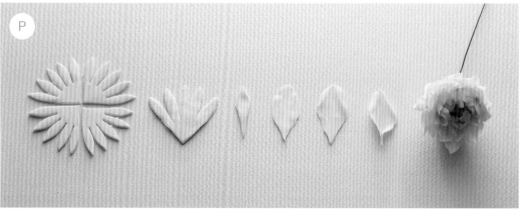

CALYX

Bud Calyx

1   Mix Holly/Ivy and White SFP at a ratio of 1:4 to make a very pale green paste. To make the upper part of the calyx, roll out some of the paste and cut out a shape with a 3.3cm or 4cm (1¹⁄₈" or 1¹⁄₂") daisy cutter.

2   Place the shape on a foam pad and draw a bone tool out from the centre and along each sepal to stretch the paste. Soften the edges using a flower shaping tool. Mark a central line inside each sepal with a leaf shaping tool (Q).

3   Thread the upper calyx up the wire then fix the sepals around the base of the bud using edible glue.

4   To make the lower part of the calyx, use the Mexican hat method on page 17 to cut out a second daisy shape with a raised centre. Shape the sepals as in step 2 above then cup the centre of the calyx with a bone tool (R).

5   Thread the lower calyx up the wire with the sepals curving downwards and attach it at the centre with edible glue.

6   Brush the calyx with a mixture of Holly/Ivy and Leaf Green dust food colours then catch the edges with Cyclamen.

Flower Calyx

1   Mix Holly/Ivy and White SFP at a ratio of 1:4 to make a very pale green paste. Roll out some of the paste and cut out six to eight sepals with each of the no. 1 and no. 2 cutters from SK Multi-Flower Cutter Set 3.

2   Soften the edges of the calyx sepals with a flower shaping tool and draw three lines down the centre of each sepal with a leaf shaping tool.

3   For the upper part of the calyx, brush the back of the larger sepals with a mixture of Holly/Ivy and Leaf Green dust food colours. Attach these sepals with edible glue so they are evenly spaced around the base of the flower.

4   For the lower part of the calyx, brush both sides of the smaller calyx sepals with a mixture of Holly/Ivy and Leaf Green dust food colours then catch the edges with Cyclamen. Attach these sepals at the base of the calyx so they are curving downwards.

LEAF

Make dahlia leaves using either the large wired petal and leaves guide on page 19, or the covered wire method below.

1 Apply a small amount of edible glue to a 24-gauge green floral wire. Roll a small ball of Pale Green SFP and thread it onto the wire. Stretch the paste along the wire by rolling it against a non-stick board with your fingers until the length is approximately 90% of the length of the leaf cutter.

2 Thinly roll out some Pale Green SFP and use a wooden skewer to indent a line in the centre of the paste. Brush a little edible glue along the indent and place the covered wire into it. Use a CelStick to roll the paste inwards on either side of the wire to ensure it is secure.

3 Cut out a leaf with a cutter from nos. 3–7 of SK Multi-Flower Cutter Set 2 with the pointed end at the top. Use a cutting wheel to cut away 2mm (1/16") from the base on either side of the leaf. Use the pointed end of the no. 1 cutter from SK Multi-Flower Cutter Set 2 to make cuts along the top edges of the leaf.

4 Press the leaf between the two halves of a dahlia leaf veiner with the wire at the back. Soften the edges with a flower shaping tool. Pinch the top and bottom of the leaf with your fingers to give it movement.

5 Brush the front of the leaf with a mixture of Leaf Green and Holly/Ivy dust food colours then catch the edges with Cyclamen. Coat the leaf with confectioners' glaze using your preferred method from the glazing guide on page 25.

6 Tape down the wire of the leaf with green floral tape.

ASSEMBLY

1 Bend the wire at the neck of the flower slightly as the flower blooms facing forward.

2 Tape the first leaf 1–2cm (3/8–3/4") under the base of the bud or flower head, starting with the smaller leaves and taping them down the stem at 3cm (1 1/8") intervals on alternate sides.

3 Tape a bud stem to the flower stem, positioning the bud higher than the flower head. Tape the larger leaves below them.

Pompon Dahlia

The Pompon dahlia is a double-flowered miniature bloom. Its spherical form is made up entirely from petals that are curved inwards. This dahlia is popular because of its lovely ball shape. I find it very satisfying to make a pompon bouquet with lots of different colours.

EDIBLES

SK Sugar Florist Paste (SFP): Holly/Ivy, Pale Green, Pale Pink and White

SK Professional Dust Food Colours: Cyclamen, Holly/Ivy, Leaf Green and Vine

SK Quality Food Colour (QFC) Dust: Pink

SK Designer Bridal Satin Dust Food Colour: White Satin

EQUIPMENT

20- and 24-gauge green floral wires

Orchard Products Six Petal Cutters: N3 and N2 (3.5cm and 4cm/1³/₈" and 1½")

SK Multi-Flower Cutter Set 1: nos. 1, 2 and 3

SK Multi-Flower Cutter Set 2: nos. 1, 3 and 4

Flat-ended tweezers

Tinkertech Two Eight Petal Pointed Daisy Cutter: no. 104 (3.3cm/1¼")

SK Great Impressions Dahlia Leaf Veiner: Large (9cm/3½")

Green floral tape

ESSENTIAL EDIBLES AND EQUIPMENT (SEE PAGE 10)

FLOWER CENTRE

1 Make a 1cm (³/₈") diameter flower base using the foundation method for a flower paste dahlia centre base on page 94.

2 Knead a small amount of White SFP into Pale Pink SFP at a ratio of 1:3 to make a light pink colour.

3 Make and attach the central petals using the foundation method on page 94 and a 3.5cm (1³/₈") six petal flower cutter (A).

4 Brush the flower centre with a little Vine dust food colour. Coat the flower centre with confectioners' glaze using your preferred method from Glazing on page 25. Set aside to dry.

PETALS

1 Roll out some light pink SFP and cut out a flower shape with a 4cm (1½") six petal cutter.

2 Place the shape on a non-stick board and use a CelStick to widen each petal. Move it to a foam pad and stretch the paste by drawing out from the centre and along each petal with a flower shaping tool.

3 Curl the edges on both sides of the petals inwards using a wooden skewer (B). Pinch the base of each petal with flat-ended tweezers (C).

4 Thread the flower shape up the wire of the flower centre then attach the petals around it with edible glue (D).

5 Make six petals using the foundation method for rolled dahlia petals on page 94, light pink SFP and the no. 1 petal cutter from SK Multi-Flower Cutter Set 1: the pointed end is at the top of the petal. Curl the pointed top edge of the petal outwards with a leaf shaping tool or your fingers (E).

6 Attach the rolled petals beneath the previous layer of petals using edible glue. Position them in the gaps, with the overlapping edge of each petal facing the previous layer (F).

7 Repeat steps 5–6 to make and attach six petals using the no. 2 petal cutter from SK Multi-Flower Cutter Set 1 (G).

8 Repeat steps 5–6 to make and attach six petals using the no. 3 petal cutter from SK Multi-Flower Cutter Set 1; at this stage the petals should sit at almost a 90° angle to the wire (H).

Tip Make the petals very thin so that each one fits neatly. If the finished flower does not have a ball shape, try to cut away a little paste at the base of the final two layers of petals, or use cutter no. 2 instead of no. 3.

9 Repeat steps 5–6 to make and attach six petals using the no. 3 petal cutter from SK Multi-Flower Cutter Set 1 but this time roll up the petals less tightly to make them slightly larger than the previous layer.

10 Repeat steps 5–6 to make and attach three more layers of six petals using the no. 3 petal cutter from SK Multi-Flower Cutter Set 1. With each layer of six petals, roll them up tighter at the base to open out the tip of the petal. This makes each layer thinner than the previous one to give the whole flower a round appearance. The lower layers of the petals should be attached almost pointing downwards (I).

11 Brush the lower half of the inside of the petals with a mixture of White Satin and Pink dust food colours. Lightly dust the centre and some edges of the petals.

CALYX

Make the calyx using the foundation method for a dahlia bud calyx on page 97.

LEAVES AND ASSEMBLY

Make the leaves with the nos. 3 and 4 cutters from SK Multi-Flower Cutter Set 2 and assemble the flower using the foundation methods on page 98.

Decorative Dahlia

WITH SINGLE-COLOUR PETALS

This flower has the presence typical of very large dahlias.
The petals of this dahlia are broad with edges that partially roll back
or forward. They are uniform and regularly arranged, tending to curve
towards the stem.

EDIBLES

SK Sugar Florist Paste (SFP): Candy Pink,
Holly/Ivy, Pale Green and White

SK Professional Dust Food Colours:
Cyclamen, Holly/Ivy, Leaf Green and Rose

SK Quality Food Colour Dust (QFC): Pink

EQUIPMENT

2cm and 2.5cm (¾" and 1") polystyrene balls

20- and 24-gauge green floral wires

26- and 28-gauge white floral wires

Orchard Products Six Petal Cutter: N1 (5cm/2")

Tinkertech Two Sunflower Cutter:
no. 673 (7cm/2¾")

Flat-ended tweezers

SK Multi-Flower Cutter Set 2: nos. 1–7

SK Multi-Flower Cutter Set 3: nos. 1 and 2

Green floral tape

Tinkertech Two Eight Petal Pointed Daisy Cutter:
no. 103 (4cm/1½")

SK Great Impressions Dahlia Leaf Veiner: Large
(9cm/3½")

ESSENTIAL EDIBLES AND EQUIPMENT (SEE PAGE 10)

FLOWER CENTRE

1 Make the flower base using the foundation method for a polystyrene dahlia centre base on page 94.

2 Make and attach the central petals using the foundation method on page 94, Candy Pink SFP and a 5cm (2") six petal flower cutter.

3 Repeat step 2 to make and attach a second flower shape to the centre, leaving the tips of the petals unattached.

4 Roll out some Candy Pink SFP slightly thicker than for the previous petals. Cut out four more flower shapes. Working on them one at a time, place each flower shape on a foam pad and draw a bone tool out from the centre and along each petal to stretch the paste. Use a leaf shaping tool to mark a central vein from the tip to the centre of each petal. Pinch the tip of each petal between your finger and thumb.

5 Thread the flower shapes up the wire of the flower centre one by one, attaching the petals with edible glue and leaving the tips upright.

6 Brush the flower centre with a mixture of Cyclamen, Rose and Pink dust food colours.

PETALS

Inner Petals

1 Roll out some Candy Pink SFP and cut out a flower shape using the sunflower cutter. Cut it into quarters so each segment has five petals.

2 Working on one segment at a time, use a bone tool to stretch each petal from the base to the tip until it is 2.5cm (1") in length. Widen each petal slightly using a CelStick then soften the edges with a flower shaping tool. Use a leaf shaping tool to mark three central lines on the inside of each petal. Pinch the base of each petal using flat-ended tweezers.

3 Brush the base of the petals with a mixture of Cyclamen, Rose and Pink dust food colours.

4 Attach the four flower segments in an evenly spaced layer around the flower centre with edible glue (A).

Outer Petals

1 Thinly roll out some Candy Pink SFP. Follow the foundation method for large wired flowers and leaves on page 19 to cut out six wired petals using 28-gauge white wires and the no. 5 cutter from SK Multi-Flower Cutter Set 2: the pointed end is the top of the petal. Cut away 2mm (¹/₁₆") from the lower part of both sides of each petal using a cutting wheel.

2 Vein and shape the petals using steps 2–3 of the foundation method for flat dahlia petals on page 94 (F). Overlap the bottom edges of each petal slightly, pinching to secure them. Use your fingers to shape both sides of the petal outwards and pinch the tip of the petal inwards (B).

3 Brush the inside base of the petals with a mixture of Cyclamen, Rose and Pink dust food colours.

4 Attach the petals around the inner petals using green floral tape, tucking the edge of each petal beneath the previous one.

5 Make four petals in each size using the foundation method for rolled dahlia petals on page 94, Candy Pink SFP and the nos. 2, 3 and 4 cutters from SK Multi-Flower Cutter Set 2, setting the pointed end at the top of the petals (C).

6 Attach the four small petals around the previous layer using edible glue. Attach the four medium petals in front of the wired outer petals made with the no. 5 cutter. Attach the large petals in between the two layers of wired petals.

7 Repeat steps 1–3 to make six wired petals using 26-gauge white wires and the no. 6 cutter from SK Multi-Flower Cutter Set 2, cutting away the very tip of each one (D). Tape the petals beneath and in between the gaps in the previous layer of wired petals, overlapping the edges.

8 Repeat step 7 to make and attach six wired petals using the no. 7 cutter (E). Curl the tips of the petals back and downwards with your fingers.

9 Repeat step 8 to make and attach the final layer of six wired petals using the no. 6 cutter (F).

Additional Petals

1 Make four or five unwired petals using steps 1–3 for the outer petals with each of the nos. 5 and 6 petal cutters. Set each petal aside in a ring of tissue paper to firm until it holds its shape (G).

2 Glue the smaller additional petals in between the inner two layers of wired petals. Attach the larger additional petals in between the outer two layers of wired petals to give balance to the flower.

CALYX AND LEAF

Make the calyx and leaf using the foundation method for a dahlia flower calyx and leaves on pages 97–98. Cut out the leaf using cutter no. 6 or 7 from SK Multi-Flower Cutter Set 2.

BUD AND ASSEMBLY

Make the buds using the foundation method for dahlia buds and a bud calyx on pages 96–97. Assemble the flower using the foundation method on page 98.

Decorative Dahlia

WITH FLECKED PETALS

The petals of this dahlia are slightly more twisted, with their arrangement appearing irregular in contrast with the previous decorative dahlia. The speckled effect on this flower looks impressive and is easy to achieve using airbrush food colour and a small spray bottle.

● ● ● ● ●

EDIBLES

SK Sugar Florist Paste (SFP): Holly/Ivy, Pale Green, Poinsettia and White

SK Professional Dust Food Colours: Cyclamen, Holly/Ivy, Leaf Green, Poinsettia and Vine

SK Designer Bridal Satin Dust Food Colour: White Satin

SK Professional Airbrush Food Colour: Carnival Red

EQUIPMENT

2cm and 2.5cm (¾" and 1") polystyrene balls

20- and 24-gauge green floral wires

26- and 28-gauge white floral wires

Orchard Products Six Petal Cutter: N1 (5cm/2")

SK Multi-Flower Cutter Set 2: nos. 1–7

SK Multi-Flower Cutter Set 3: nos. 1 and 2

Green floral tape

Small spray bottle

SK High-Quality Paintbrush: no. 00

Tinkertech Two Sunflower Cutter: no. 673 (7cm/2¾")

Tinkertech Two Eight Petal Pointed Daisy Cutter: no. 103 (4cm/1½")

SK Great Impressions Dahlia Leaf Veiner: Large (9cm/3½")

ESSENTIAL EDIBLES AND EQUIPMENT (SEE PAGE 10)

FLOWER CENTRE

1 Make the flower base using the foundation method for a polystyrene dahlia centre base on page 94.

2 Make and attach the central petals using the foundation method on page 94, White SFP and a 5cm (2") six petal flower cutter (A).

3 Repeat step 2 to attach a second flower shape to the centre. Lightly brush the flower centre with a little Vine dust food colour.

4 Roll out some White SFP slightly thicker than for the previous petals. Cut out four more flower shapes. Working on them one at a time, place each flower shape on a foam pad and draw a bone tool out from the centre and along each petal to stretch the paste. Use a leaf shaping tool to mark a central vein from the tip to the centre of each petal. Pinch the tip of each petal between your finger and thumb.

5 Brush the whole of each flower shape lightly with White Satin dust food colour and dust the centres with Vine. Thread the flower shapes up the wire of the flower centre one by one, attaching the petals around the centre with edible glue and leaving the tips upright (B).

PETALS

Inner Petals

1 Thinly roll out some White SFP and cut out four petals using the no. 1 petal cutter from SK Multi-Flower Cutter Set 2. Place the petals on a foam pad and use a flower shaping tool to soften the edges and stretch the tip of each petal. Roll the petals using steps 2–3 of the foundation method for rolled dahlia petals on page 94.

2 Attach the rolled petals beneath the previous layer of central petals using edible glue. Position them in the gaps, with the overlapped edge of each petal facing the previous layer.

3 Thinly roll out some White SFP and cut out four petals using the no. 2 petal cutter from SK Multi-Flower Cutter Set 2. Mark three lines along the centre of the petal following step 2 of the foundation method for flat dahlia petals on page 94.

4 Flip the petals over onto a foam pad and soften the edges with a flower shaping tool. Run a leaf shaping tool, at an angle, down the top edge on either side of each petal to stretch the tip and curve the edges. Flip the petals over again and roll them using steps 2–3 of the foundation method for rolled dahlia petals on page 94.

5 Repeat steps 3–4 to make four petals using the no. 3 petal cutter from SK Multi-Flower Cutter Set 2 (C).

6 Attach the petals made using cutter nos. 2 and 3 below the previous layer, in between the gaps. Use your fingers to give the petals movement while they are still semi-dry.

7 Brush all of the inner petals lightly with White Satin dust food colour and dust the base of the petals with Vine.

Outer Petals

1 Follow the foundation method for large wired petals and leaves on page 19 to cut out six wired petals using 28-gauge white floral wires and the no. 4 petal cutter from SK Multi-Flower Cutter Set 2: five with White SFP and one with Poinsettia SFP.

2 Vein and soften the petals using steps 2–3 of the foundation method for flat dahlia petals on page 94. Run a leaf shaping tool, at an angle, down the top edge on either side of each petal to curve the edges. Turn the petals over again and use a flower shaping tool to pull the centre of the top edge upwards. Overlap the bottom edges of each petal slightly with your fingers, pinching to secure them.

3 Brush the white petals lightly with White Satin dust food colour. Add a little Vine at the base. Use Poinsettia dust food colour to dust the red petal.

4 Attach the petals around the flower and in between the previous layer of petals using green floral tape, tucking the edges of the petals underneath one another.

5 Repeat steps 1–4 to make and attach six petals using the no. 5 petal cutter, positioning the red petal behind the red one in the previous layer (D).

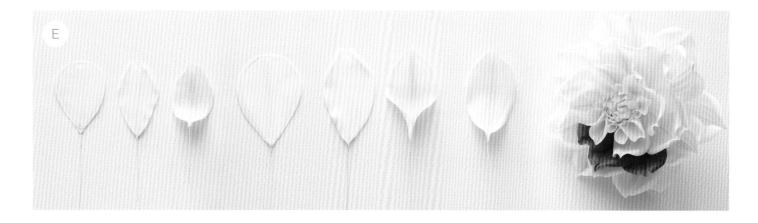

6 Repeat step 5 to make and attach a third layer of six wired petals but cut away 2–3mm ($^{1}/_{16}$–$^{1}/_{8}$") from both sides of each one to make the petals thinner before veining them. Instead of overlapping the edges at the base of the petal, just pinch the base slightly.

7 Repeat step 6 to make and attach a fourth layer of six white petals using 26-gauge white wires and the no. 6 cutter from SK Multi-Flower Cutter Set 2, overlapping the edges at the base of the petal.

8 Repeat step 7 to make the final layer of six white petals but instead of overlapping the edges at the base of the petal, just pinch the bottom slightly. Attach the final layer of petals (E).

Additional Petals

1 Make four or five unwired white petals using steps 1–3 for the outer petals on page 117 and the no. 5 cutter from SK Multi-Flower Cutter Set 2. Set each petal aside in a ring of tissue paper until it holds its shape.

2 Use edible glue to attach the additional petals in between the second and third layers of outer petals to give balance to the flower.

COLOURING THE FLOWER

1 Transfer some Carnival Red airbrush colour to a small spray bottle and use it to spray the flower from a distance to give a speckled effect.

2 Mix some Poinsettia dust food colour with clear alcohol to make a paint. Use a no. 1 paintbrush to paint thin red lines up the centre of some of the petals. Brush a little Poinsettia dust food colour onto the petals if needed.

CALYX AND LEAF

Make the calyx and leaf using the foundation method for a dahlia flower calyx and leaf on pages 97–98. Cut out the leaf using cutter no. 6 or 7 from SK Multi-Flower Cutter Set 2.

BUD AND ASSEMBLY

Make the buds using the foundation method for dahlia buds and a bud calyx on pages 96–97. Assemble the flower using the foundation method on page 98.

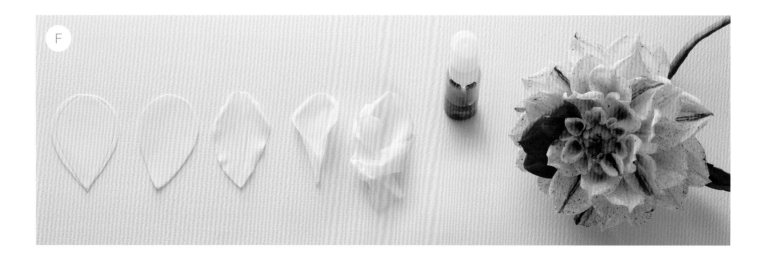

The fiery reds and fresh greens of this arrangement would make a beautiful winter bouquet.

Semi-Cactus Dahlia

This form of dahlia has double flowers with long, pointed petals which are broad at the base and curve backwards for up to half of their length. I have chosen to make a semi-cactus dahlia with ruffled petals as it looks more attractive in flower arrangements.

• • • •

EDIBLES

SK Sugar Florist Paste (SFP): Holly/Ivy, Pale Green, Pale Yellow, Soft Peach and White

SK Professional Dust Food Colours: Cyclamen, Daffodil, Holly/Ivy, Leaf Green and Rose

SK Quality Food Colour (QFC) Dust: Pink

EQUIPMENT

2cm and 2.5cm (¾" and 1") polystyrene balls

20- and 24-gauge green floral wires

28- and 30-gauge white floral wires

Orchard Products Six Petal Cutter: N1 (5cm/2")

SK Multi-Flower Cutter Set 2: nos. 1, 2, 6 and 7

SK Multi-Flower Cutter Set 3: nos. 1–6

Green floral tape

Tinkertech Two Sunflower Cutter: no. 673 (7cm/2¾")

Tinkertech Two Eight Petal Pointed Daisy Cutter: no. 103 (4cm/1½")

SK Great Impressions Dahlia Leaf Veiner: Large (9cm/3½")

ESSENTIAL EDIBLES AND EQUIPMENT (SEE PAGE 10)

FLOWER CENTRE

1 Make the flower base using the foundation method for a polystyrene dahlia centre base on page 94.

2 Knead a small amount of Soft Peach SFP into Pale Yellow SFP at a ratio of 1:9 to create a golden yellow colour.

3 Make and attach the central petals using the foundation method for central petals on page 94, golden yellow SFP and a 5cm (2") six petal flower cutter.

4 Repeat step 3 to make and attach three more flower shapes to the centre one by one, leaving the tips of the petals unattached.

5 Brush the top of the flower centre with a mixture of Cyclamen, Rose and Pink dust food colours.

PETALS

Inner Petals

1 Roll out some golden yellow SFP slightly thicker than for the flower centre petals and cut out a shape with the six petal cutter. Place the shape on a non-stick board and widen each petal using a CelStick. Separate the shape into six individual petals using a cutting wheel.

2 Soften the edges of the petals with a flower shaping tool on a foam pad. Use a leaf shaping tool to mark three central lines down each petal.

3 Brush the centre of each petal with a mixture of Cyclamen, Rose and Pink dust food colours. Roll the petals following steps 2–3 of the foundation method for rolled dahlia petals on page 94 (A).

4 Attach the petals around the flower centre with edible glue so they are evenly spaced, with the overlapping edge at the base of the petal facing the flower centre.

5 Thinly roll out some golden yellow SFP and cut out six petals using the no. 2 cutter from SK Multi-Flower Cutter Set 3. Shape and colour the petals as in steps 2–3 above and attach them around and in between the gaps of the previous layer (B).

Outer Petals

1 Thinly roll out some golden yellow SFP and follow the foundation method for large wired petals and leaves on page 19 to cut out three wired petals using 30-gauge white floral wires and the no. 3 cutter from SK Multi-Flower Cutter Set 3.

2 Vein and shape the petals using steps 2–3 of the foundation method for flat dahlia petals on page 94. Overlap the bottom edges of each petal slightly, pinching to secure them. Use your fingers to shape both sides of the petal outwards and pinch the tip of the petal inwards.

3 Brush the entire surface of the petals lightly with Daffodil dust food colour and dust the inside base of the petal with a mixture of Pink and Cyclamen dust food colours (C).

4 Repeat steps 1–3 to make three petals using the no. 4 cutter.

5 Attach the three smaller wired petals around the inner petals of the flower with green floral tape so they are evenly spaced. Attach the three larger petals in between them. Brush a small amount of edible glue on the neck of the petals to secure them if needed.

6 Make six wired petals as in steps 1–3 using 28-gauge white wires and the no. 5 cutter. Attach the petals around the previous layer of petals.

7 Repeat step 6 to make 12 wired petals using the no. 6 cutter, attaching them in two layers of six petals (D).

8 Repeat step 6 but use the no. 6 cutter and widen the petals using a CelStick before veining and shaping them. Curl the tips of the petals back and downwards with your fingers before attaching them to the flower (E).

9 Make and attach a final layer of six wired petals as in step 8 using the no. 5 cutter (F).

Additional Petals

1 Make several unwired petals following steps 1–3 for the outer petals: three or four petals with each of the nos. 3 and 4 cutters and eight to 10 petals with the no. 5 cutter from SK Multi-Flower Cutter Set 3. Set each petal aside in a ring of tissue paper to firm until it holds its shape (G).

2 Use edible glue to attach the two smaller sizes of additional petals in front of or behind the first layer of wired petals. Attach the larger additional petals where needed between the outer four layers of wired petals to give balance to the flower.

CALYX AND LEAF

Make the calyx and leaf using the foundation method for a dahlia flower calyx and leaf on pages 97–98. Cut out the leaf using cutter no. 6 or 7 from SK Multi-Flower Cutter Set 2.

BUD AND ASSEMBLY

Make the bud using the foundation method for dahlia buds and a bud calyx on pages 96–97. Assemble the flower using the method on page 98.

Collarette Dahlia

Collarette dahlias have blooms with a single outer ring of petals and a ring of small petals in the centre forming the 'collar'. I love the combination of colours in this particular sugar flower.

EDIBLES

SK Sugar Florist Paste (SFP): Holly/Ivy, Pale Green, Pale Yellow, Poinsettia and White

SK Professional Dust Food Colours: Cyclamen, Daffodil, Holly/Ivy, Leaf Green, Rose and Vine

SK Designer Pollen Dust Food Colour: Pale Golden

SK Designer Bridal Satin Dust Food Colour: White Satin

EQUIPMENT

SK Great Impressions Daisy Centre Mould: Small (1.1cm/³/₈")

24-gauge green floral wires

28- and 30-gauge white floral wires

Small matt white pointed-head stamens

Green and white floral tape

Orchard Products Six Petal Cutters: N1 and N7 (5cm and 1.5cm/2" and ⁵/₈")

SK Multi-Flower Cutter Set 2: nos. 1, 3, 4 and 5

SK Multi-Flower Cutter Set 3: nos. 1 and 2

Tinkertech Two Eight Petal Pointed Daisy Cutter: no. 103 (4cm/1½")

Tinkertech Two Sunflower Cutter: no. 673 (7cm/2¾")

SK Great Impressions Dahlia Leaf Veiner: Large (9cm/3½")

ESSENTIAL EDIBLES AND EQUIPMENT (SEE PAGE 10)

FLOWER CENTRE

1 Form a small ball of Pale Yellow SFP into a teardrop shape then push the wider end into the daisy mould. Brush the end of a hooked 24-gauge green floral wire with edible glue and insert it into the back of the teardrop then remove the flower centre from the mould.

2 While the paste is semi-dry, use fine scissors to cut away any excess paste below the flower centre to give it a very thin neck. Set aside to dry.

3 Brush the top of the flower centre with Daffodil dust food colour (A).

4 Fold four white pointed-head stamens in half and attach them to the hooked end of a 30-gauge white floral wire. Use white floral tape to tape down the wire, starting 1.5cm (⁵⁄₈") below the anthers. Brush the stamens and the taped wire with Daffodil dust food colour. Brush a little edible glue on the anthers and dip them into a small pot filled with Pale Golden pollen dust food colour (B).

5 Repeat step 4 to make 15 bunches of stamens. Bend the neck of each bunch with pliers to fit around the flower centre. Position the top of the taped section of the stamen wires just below the top of the flower centre, securing them with green floral tape around the stem.

6 Roll out some Pale Yellow SFP and cut out five or six flower shapes using the 1.5cm (⁵⁄₈") six petal cutter. Place the flower shapes on a foam pad and use a leaf shaping tool to mark a central vein down each petal. Cup the flower shapes using a small ball tool.

7 Attach the cupped flower shapes in between the daisy centre and the stamens with edible glue. Brush them with Daffodil dust food colour (C).

PETALS

Inner Petals

1 Make 10 petals following the guide to making small wired petals and leaves on page 19 and using steps 1–3 of the foundation method for flat dahlia petals on page 94. Use 28-gauge white floral wires, White SFP and the no. 2 petal cutter from SK Multi-Flower Cutter Set 3: the pointed end is the tip of the petal.

2 Use a cutting wheel to make a deep cut on the right side, left side or both sides of each petal so you have a selection of each type (D).

3 Place the petals upside down on a foam pad and curl the edge of the petals backwards using a leaf shaping tool. Pinch the base and the tip of each petal to create movement. Brush the entire surface of each petal with White Satin dust food colour. Add a little Vine to the centre of the base (E).

4 Attach the petals around the flower centre using green floral tape so they are evenly spaced (F).

Outer Petals

1 Thinly roll out some Poinsettia SFP. Follow the guide to making large wired petals and leaves on page 19 to cut out eight wired petals using 28-gauge white wires and the no. 5 cutter from SK Multi-Flower Cutter Set 2.

2 Working on them one by one, place the petals face down on a foam pad and soften the edges with a ball tool. Use a flower shaping tool to give the edges a gentle wave then stretch the tip upwards.

3 Mark a central vein with a bamboo skewer. Turn the petal over and use a leaf shaping tool to mark three lines on either side of the central vein.

4 Use your fingers to curve the very edges of the petal backwards then pinch the tip and base of the petal. Brush the petal with a mixture of Rose and Cyclamen dust food colours (G).

5 Attach four of the outer petals around the inner petals with green floral tape. Tape the remaining four petals behind and in between them.

6 Make several white petals as in steps 1–3 for the inner petals but without a wire, using the no. 1 petal cutter from SK Multi-Flower Cutter Set 3 and dusting the base with Cyclamen dust food colour (H). Attach them in between the inner and outer petals using edible glue.

CALYX

1 Knead some White SFP into Holly/Ivy SFP to create a light leaf green colour. Roll out some light leaf green SFP and cut out a flower shape using the daisy cutter. Place the flower shape on a foam pad and use a bone tool to stretch each sepal. Use a flower shaping tool to smooth the edges.

2 Cut each sepal in half with fine scissors (I). Curl each half sepal inwards by drawing a leaf shaping tool from the tip into the centre. Use a cutting wheel to separate the flower shape into eight individual split sepals (J).

3 Attach the calyx sepals in between the inner and outer petals using edible glue.

4 Repeat step 1 to make a second flower shape then use a cutting wheel to separate it into eight individual sepals (K). Attach these calyx sepals around the wire at the back of the flower with edible glue, with the tips facing downwards.

5 Lightly brush the edges of the calyx sepals with Cyclamen dust food colour.

BUD

Make the bud using the 5cm (2") six petal cutter and the foundation method for a small dahlia bud and bud calyx on pages 96–97.

LEAVES AND ASSEMBLY

Make the leaves using cutters nos. 3–5 from SK Multi-Flower Cutter Set 2 and assemble the flower using the foundation methods on page 98.

Anemone-Flowered Dahlia

The blooms of anemone-flowered dahlias have one or more outer rings of generally flat petals surrounding a dense group of tubular petals in the centre. Make sure there is a good balance between the central petals and the outer ring; if the centre becomes too dominant it can look like a pincushion flower.

● ● ● ● ●

EDIBLES

SK Sugar Florist Paste (SFP): Holly/Ivy, Pale Green, Pale Yellow and White

SK Professional Dust Food Colours: Cyclamen, Daffodil, Holly/Ivy, Leaf Green and Vine

SK Designer Bridal Satin Dust Food Colour: White Satin

EQUIPMENT

SK Great Impressions Daisy Centre Mould: Small (1.1cm/³/₈")

20- and 24-gauge green floral wires

28-gauge white floral wires

Tinkertech Two Eight Petal Pointed Daisy Cutters: nos. 103 and 104 (4cm and 3.3cm/ 1½" and 1¼")

Flat-ended tweezers

SK Multi-Flower Cutter Set 2: nos. 1, 3, 4 and 5

Green floral tape

Tinkertech Two Sunflower Cutter: no. 673 (7cm/2¾")

SK Great Impressions Dahlia Leaf Veiner: Large (9cm/3½")

ESSENTIAL EDIBLES AND EQUIPMENT (SEE PAGE 10)

FLOWER CENTRE

1 Form a small ball of Pale Yellow SFP and push it into the daisy mould. Brush the end of a hooked 20-gauge green floral wire with edible glue and insert it into the back of the ball then remove the flower centre from the mould. Set aside to dry completely.

2 Brush the top of the flower centre with Daffodil dust food colour.

3 Roll out some Pale Yellow SFP and cut out a flower shape using the 3.3cm (1¼") daisy cutter. Place the shape on a non-stick board and widen each petal using a CelStick. Use a flower shaping tool to stretch the tips.

4 Curl the edges on both sides of each petal inwards using a bamboo skewer then pinch the base of each petal with flat-ended tweezers.

5 Repeat steps 3–4 to make a second flower shape using the 4cm (1½") daisy cutter. Thread the flower shapes up the wire of the flower centre, one by one with the smallest first, and attach the petals around the centre with edible glue, leaving the tips upright (A).

6 Repeat steps 3–4 to make four more flower shapes using the 4cm (1½") daisy cutter. Brush a little edible glue at the centre of each shape and fold it in half, then apply a little more glue and fold it in half again. Pinch the pointed base of the petal segment with your fingers (B). Attach the four petal segments around the flower centre with edible glue so they are evenly spaced.

7 Repeat step 6 to make four more petal segments and attach them in between the previous layer of segments (C).

8 Repeat steps 6–7 to make and attach two layers of four petal segments using the 3.3cm (1¼") daisy cutter. Brush the flower centre with Daffodil dust food colour, with stronger colour at the centre (D).

OUTER PETALS

1 Thinly roll out some White SFP. Follow the guide to making large wired petals and leaves on page 19 to cut out eight wired petals using 28-gauge white floral wires and the no. 5 petal cutter from SK Multi-Flower Cutter Set 2.

2 Vein and shape the petals using steps 2–3 of the foundation method for flat dahlia petals on page 94. Use a flower shaping tool to stretch the top edge at the centre of each petal upwards then pinch the tip with your fingers.

3 Curl the edge on both sides of each petal backwards with your fingers then pinch the base of the petal inwards. Brush the whole petal lightly with White Satin dust food colour then brush a little Vine dust food colour up the centre from the base of the petal (E).

4 Attach four petals around the flower centre using green floral tape so they are evenly spaced. Tape the remaining four petals around and in between them (F).

5 Combine a small amount of Pale Yellow SFP with White SFP to make a marbled yellow paste. Thinly roll out some of the marbled yellow SFP and cut out eight unwired petals using the no. 3 petal cutter. Use a cutting wheel to make two deep 'V' shaped cuts in each petal to create a set of three small petals.

6 Smooth the edges of the petals using a flower shaping tool then curl them by drawing a leaf shaping tool up the centre of each one. Brush the petals with White Satin dust food colour then apply a little Vine at the centre. Pinch the base of each set of three petals (G).

7 Attach the petal segments in between the flower centre and the wired petals with edible glue (H, see overleaf).

CALYX

1 Knead some White SFP into Holly/Ivy SFP to create a light leaf green colour. Roll out some light leaf green SFP and cut out two flower shapes using the 4cm (1½") daisy cutter. Working on one at a time, place the flower shapes on a foam pad. Use a bone tool to stretch each petal then use a flower shaping tool to smooth the edges. Use a cutting wheel to separate each flower shape into eight individual sepals.

2 Attach eight calyx sepals around the wire at the back of the flower with edible glue, with the tips facing upwards for the upper calyx. Attach the remaining eight calyx petals curved downwards for the lower calyx.

3 Brush the calyces with Leaf Green dust food colour and catch the edges with Cyclamen.

BUD

Make the buds using the foundation method for a small dahlia bud and bud calyx on pages 96–97.

LEAF AND ASSEMBLY

Make the leaf using cutter no. 4 or 5 from SK Multi-Flower Cutter Set 2 and assemble the flower using the foundation methods on page 98.

Tulip

Tulips can be divided into 15 groups based on their
flower characteristics. This chapter includes single late,
lily-flowered, parrot, fringed and double-flowered tulips.
The tulip's long neck underneath its flower head will
allow you to add attractive lines and natural movement
to sugar flower arrangements.

Tulip Foundations

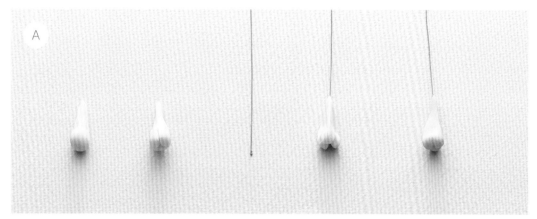

PISTIL

1 Roll some Pale Yellow SFP into a teardrop shape which is approximately 2.5cm (1") long. Make three evenly spaced cuts in the wider end of the shape using fine scissors. Slightly open the top of the pistil with your fingers.

2 Brush a small amount of edible glue onto a 28-gauge hooked green floral wire. Insert it into the central tip of the pistil and pull it through so the hooked end of the wire is embedded in the paste.

3 Use a flower shaping tool to give the cone-shaped neck of the pistil three flat sides. Brush the stigma with Daffodil dust food colour and the style with Vine. Leave it to dry (A).

STAMENS

1 Roll some Pale Yellow SFP into a sausage between your finger and thumb until it is approximately 2.5cm (1") long and tapered at both ends. Insert a glued 30-gauge white wire into one end.

2 Push a flower shaping tool into the paste to create a hollow down the length of the stamen. Bring the sides around to close the centre. Pinch and twist the tip with your finger and thumb.

3 Dust the anthers with Daffodil dust food colour. For brown anthers, paint a mixture of Bulrush dust food colour and clear alcohol over the Daffodil dust. Leave patches of yellow for a more natural look.

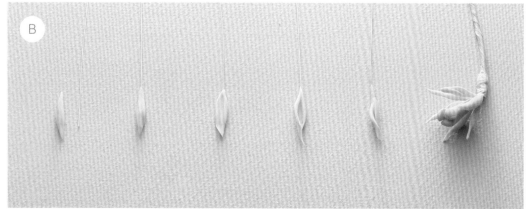

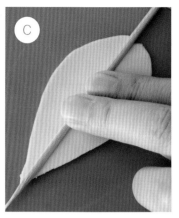
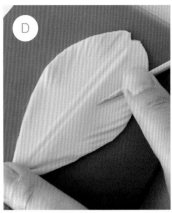
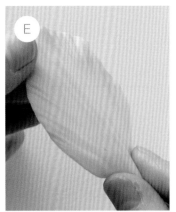
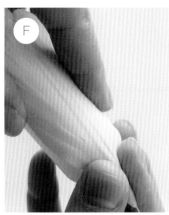

4 Repeat steps 1–3 to make six stamens in total. Leave them to dry. Tape the stamens around the pistil one by one using the same colour floral tape as the stem.

PETALS

1 Cut out the wired petals using the large wired petals and leaves guide on page 19, the specified petal cutter and the specified floral wire.

2 Mark three lines in the middle of the petal by pressing down with a bamboo skewer: one along the central vein and one on either side (C).

3 Vein the petal by rolling a bamboo skewer along the edge on either side of the central vein, keeping the tip of the tool pointing towards the base of the petal (D). Alternatively, you could use a specifically-designed tulip petal veiner. Soften the edge of the petal with a flower shaping tool on the unveined side of the petal.

4 Dust the petal with the specified dust food colour. Pinch together 1.5–2cm (⅝–¾") of the base of the petal around the wire (E).

5 Lay the petal over the end of a small rolling pin with the veined side facing outwards. Adjust the petal to give it a cupped shape (F). Press the base of the petal tightly around the wire (G). Bend the wire and curve the base of the petal around the shape of the rolling pin (H). Bend the wire back again then remove the excess paste from around the base (I).

6 Curl the upper edges of the petal around into the inside using a bamboo skewer or your fingers.

7 Attach the petals to the base of the flower centre using floral tape with the veined side facing outwards (J).

STEM

For a tulip flower, tape a 22-gauge green floral wire under the base of the flower to strengthen the stem. Wrap thin strips of kitchen paper around the wires then tape it again to make the stem thicker. For a bud, simply wrap thin strips of kitchen paper around the wire before taping it. Brush Leaf Green dust food colour around the base of the flower and the tape.

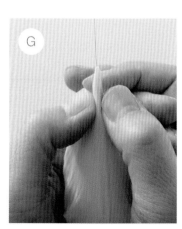
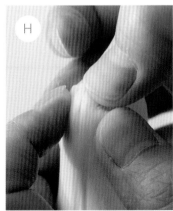
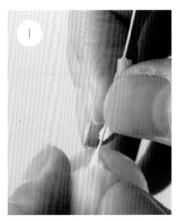

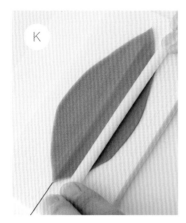

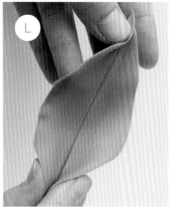

LEAF

Make tulip leaves using either the large wired petals and leaves guide on page 19, or the covered wire method below.

1   Brush a small amount of edible glue onto a 24-gauge green floral wire. Roll a small ball of Pale Green SFP and push the wire into it. Place it on a non-stick board then use your hands to roll and stretch the paste down the wire until it is approximately 90% of the length of the chosen cutter (see step 3).

2   Thinly roll out another piece of SFP. Indent a line into the paste for the central vein using a bamboo skewer. Brush a small amount of edible glue into the dent and press the covered wire into it. Secure the paste together by rolling it out with a CelStick on either side of the wire.

3   Cut out a wired leaf of a similar size to the petals using cutter no. 7, 8 or 9 from SK Multi-Flower Cutter Set 3 with the most pointed end at the top of the leaf. Use a smaller cutter for upper leaves and a larger cutter for lower leaves. Alternatively, cut them out freehand.

4   Vein the leaf with a Corn Husk texture mat: place the leaf on the mat with the wired side facing up then roll out the paste on either side of the wire with a CelStick (K).

5   Smooth the edges with a flower shaping tool. Pinch the leaf at the top and bottom to shape it (L).

6   Dust the veined side of the leaf with a mixture of Leaf Green and Holly/Ivy dust food colours then catch the edges with Cyclamen. Pass the leaf through steam to set the colour then leave it to dry (M).

ASSEMBLY

A tulip flower blooms on a long, single stem with leaves at the lower end. It looks beautiful with the long neck on show; make sure you add a slight curve to the stem for a natural look.

1   To assemble the flower, make a smaller leaf with no wire in the same way as the leaf opposite. Create a hollow at the bottom of the leaf and curve both sides upwards with your fingers.

2   Attach the leaf to the middle of the stem with glue while it is semi-dry. The leaf should follow the line of the stem.

3   Once the smaller leaf has set in place, tape around the bottom of the leaf to secure it. Continue to tape down the stem, adding two to five wired leaves around it. The hollows at the bottom of the wired leaves should fit around the stem.

Single Late Tulip

This pale pink *Tulipa* 'Pink Diamond' is in the single late group, which blooms in late spring after other types of tulip have faded. They are among the tallest tulips and have cup- or goblet-shaped flowers. Simply beautiful, this bloom will go well with any celebration.

EDIBLES

SK Sugar Florist Paste (SFP): Pale Green, Pale Pink, Pale Yellow and White

SK Professional Dust Food Colours: Cyclamen, Daffodil, Holly/Ivy, Leaf Green and Vine

SK Designer Bridal Satin Dust Food Colour: White Satin

SK Quality Food Colour (QFC) Dust: Pink

EQUIPMENT

22-, 24- and 28-gauge green floral wires

26- and 30-gauge white floral wires

Pale green floral tape

SK Multi-Flower Cutter Set 2: nos. 6, 7 and 8

SK Multi-Flower Cutter Set 3: nos. 6, 7, 8 and 9

SK Tulip Petal Cutter Set of 2

3cm x 4cm and 4cm x 5cm (1^1/$_8$" x 1^1/$_2$" and 1^1/$_2$" x 2") polystyrene ovoids

SK Great Impressions Corn Husk Textured Mat

ESSENTIAL EDIBLES AND EQUIPMENT (SEE PAGE 10)

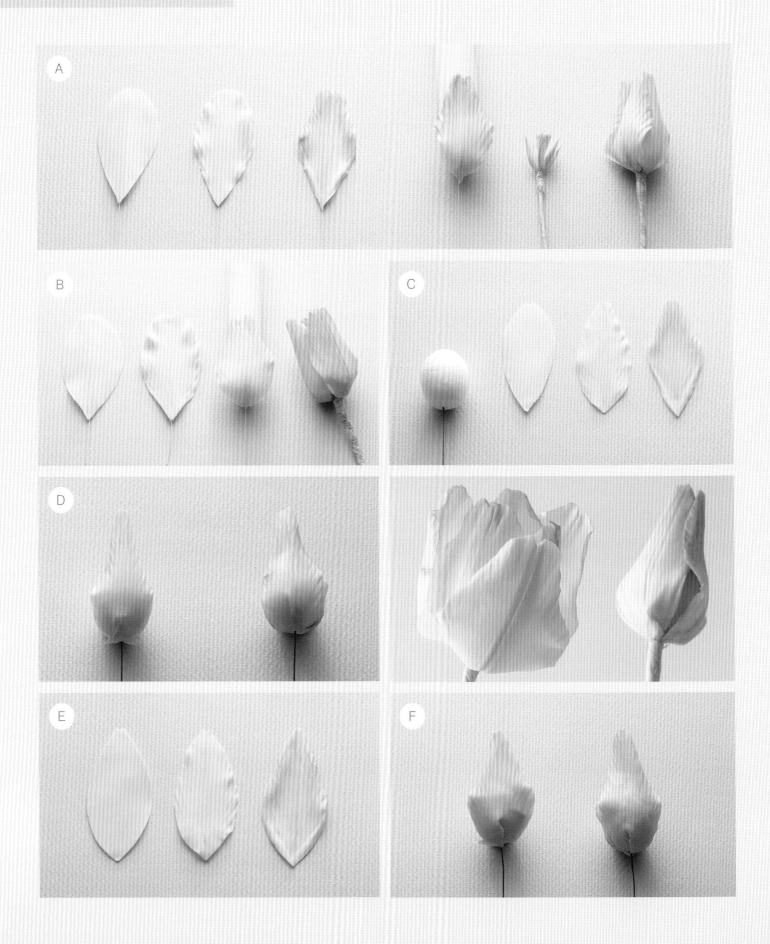

FLOWER CENTRE

Make the flower centre using the foundation method for a tulip pistil and stamens on pages 142–143. Dust the anthers with Daffodil dust food colour in step 3 for the stamens.

PETALS

1 Knead a small amount of Pale Pink SFP into White SFP to create a very pale pink colour.

2 Make three inner petals using the foundation method for tulip petals on page 143, 26-gauge white wires and very pale pink SFP. Cut out the petals using the smaller cutter from the SK Tulip Petal Cutter Set of 2. Brush the entire surface of each petal lightly with White Satin dust food colour, then brush the top edges with Pink and the base of the petal with Vine dust food colour. Attach the petals around the flower centre one by one using pale green floral tape (A).

3 Repeat step 2 to make three outer petals using the larger cutter from the SK Tulip Petal Cutter Set of 2. Attach the outer petals to the flower one at a time so the centre of each petal covers a join in the previous layer (B).

BUD

Closed Bud

1 Make a base for the bud using the polystyrene flower base guide on page 19, a 22-gauge green wire and a 3cm x 4cm (1¹⁄₈" x 1¹⁄₂") polystyrene ovoid.

2 Thinly roll out some very pale pink SFP and cut out a petal using the no. 6 petal cutter from SK Multi-Flower Cutter Set 3 with the pointed end at the top of the petal. Use a cutting wheel to make a 1cm (³⁄₈") cut up the centre from the base of the petal.

3 Texture the petal following steps 2–3 of the foundation method for tulip petals on page 143.

4 Use the pointed end of the cutter to cut away a tiny 'V' at the top of the petal then curl the top edges of the petals inwards.

5 Dust the outside of the petal with the same colours as the flower petals (C).

6 Attach the petal to the polystyrene bud base using edible glue, with the cut paste at the base of each petal sitting around the wire so the petal fits around the shape of the polystyrene ovoid from bottom to top. Cut away any excess paste from both sides of the base of the petal (D).

7 Repeat steps 2–6 to make two more petals and attach them to the bud base, overlapping slightly at the top to hide the polystyrene.

 Use a very small amount of edible glue to attach each petal to the bud base so the rough surface of the polystyrene doesn't become visible through the paste.

8 Repeat steps 2–7 to make three outer petals: use the no. 6 cutter from SK Multi-Flower Cutter Set 2 and make the central cut at the base of the petal 1.5cm (⁵⁄₈") long (E).

9 Attach the outer petals in between and slightly higher than the inner petals, securing them around the bud shape from top to bottom (F).

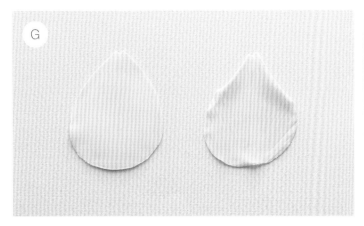

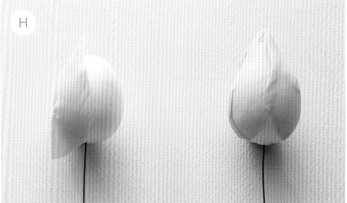

Opening Bud

1 Make a base for the bud using the polystyrene flower base guide on page 19, a 22-gauge green wire and a 4cm x 5cm (1½" x 2") polystyrene ovoid.

2 Cut out, shape and colour the petal following steps 2–5 for the closed bud on the previous page. Use the no. 7 cutter from SK Multi-Flower Cutter Set 2 and omit the cut at the petal base (G).

3 Place the petal over one side of the polystyrene bud base. Fit the petal to the base from top to bottom and pull together both sides of the excess paste at the centre base of the petal. Fold the excess paste to one side and cut it away with fine scissors. Smooth the cut edges with your finger.

4 Repeat steps 2–3 to make and attach two more petals. Wrap the petals together slightly at the top to hide the polystyrene base (H).

5 Repeat steps 2–4 to make three outer petals using the no. 8 cutter from SK Multi-Flower Cutter Set 2 (I). Attach the outer petals slightly higher than the inner petals using the same method, making sure the centre of each petal covers a join in the previous layer (J).

STEM, LEAVES AND ASSEMBLY

Make the stem and leaves and assemble the tulip using the foundation methods on pages 143–144.

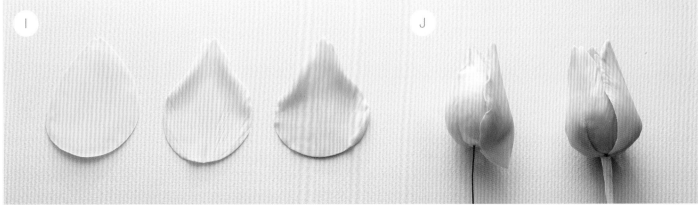

Lily-Flowered Tulip

Tulipa 'Ballerina' is a lily-flowered tulip, also known as fluted tulips. Its soft tangerine-orange, slender flowers have a sweet fragrance. Shape the centre so it is quite slim and roll out the petals thinly to make this tulip look like its graceful namesake.

EDIBLES

SK Sugar Florist Paste (SFP): Pale Green, Pale Yellow, Soft Peach and White

SK Professional Dust Food Colours: Cyclamen, Daffodil, Fuchsia, Holly/Ivy, Leaf Green and Vine

SK Designer Bridal Satin Dust Food Colour: White Satin

EQUIPMENT

22-, 24- and 28-gauge green floral wires

28- and 30-gauge white floral wires

Moss green floral tape

SK Multi-Flower Cutter Set 3: nos. 5, 6, 7, 8 and 9

SK Great Impressions Corn Husk Textured Mat

ESSENTIAL EDIBLES AND EQUIPMENT (SEE PAGE 10)

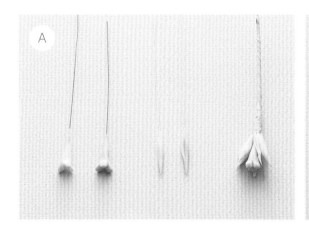

FLOWER CENTRE

Make the flower centre using the foundation method for a tulip pistil and stamens on pages 142–143. Dust the anthers with Daffodil dust food colour in step 3 for the stamens (A).

PETALS

1 Knead a small amount of Soft Peach SFP into White SFP to create a very pale peach colour.

2 Make three inner petals using the foundation method for tulip petals on page 143, 28-gauge white wires, very pale peach SFP and the no. 5 cutter from SK Multi-Flower Cutter Set 3. Brush the whole petals lightly with White Satin and Daffodil dust food colours. Brush the top edges with a mixture of Fuchsia and Daffodil and the central vein of the petal with Vine dust food colour. Draw your fingers up the petal to give it a pointed shape.

3 Attach the petals around the flower centre one by one using pale green floral tape (B).

4 Repeat step 2 to make three outer petals using the no. 6 cutter. Attach the outer petals to the flower one by one using pale green floral tape, making sure the centre of each one covers a join in the previous layer (C).

 Tip Vary the positioning of the petals from flower to flower; open out the petals for a flower in full bloom or close the petals around the stamens for a flower that is just opening.

STEM, LEAVES AND ASSEMBLY

Make the stem and leaves and assemble the tulip using the foundation methods on pages 143–144.

Parrot Tulip

Parrot tulips have serrated petals and irregular shaped blooms. As the flower matures and opens, it resembles a parrot's plumage. This group of tulips has a huge variety of colours and shapes. I recommend using pure white parrot tulips to enhance a wedding cake arrangement.

EDIBLES

SK Sugar Florist Paste (SFP): Pale Green, Holly/Ivy, Pale Yellow, Poinsettia and White

SK Professional Dust Food Colours: Daffodil, Bulrush, Cyclamen, Holly/Ivy, Leaf Green, Poinsettia and Vine

SK Designer Bridal Satin Dust Food Colour: White Satin

EQUIPMENT

22-, 24- and 28-gauge green floral wires

26- and 30-gauge white floral wires

Moss green floral tape

SK Multi-Flower Cutter Set 2: nos. 1, 7 and 8

SK Multi-Flower Cutter Set 3: nos. 7, 8 and 9

4cm x 5cm (1½" x 2") polystyrene ovoids

SK Great Impressions Corn Husk Textured Mat

ESSENTIAL EDIBLES AND EQUIPMENT (SEE PAGE 10)

FLOWER CENTRE

Make the flower centre using the foundation method for a tulip pistil and stamens on pages 142–143. Paint the anthers with a mixture of Bulrush dust food colour and clear alcohol in step 3 for the stamens (A).

PETALS

1 Thinly roll out some White SFP and cut out a 5cm x 10cm (2" x 4") rectangle. Repeat with Poinsettia SFP. Place a 26-gauge white floral wire along the long edge of one sheet, attaching it with a small amount of edible glue (B). Lay the edge of the other rectangle of paste over the wire and secure them together by smoothing the paste with your finger. Cut out a petal using the no. 8 cutter from SK Multi-Flower Cutter Set 2 (C).

2 Make small cuts along the top edge of the petal using the pointed end of the no. 1 cutter from SK Multi-Flower Cutter Set 2. Vein the petal using steps 2–3 of the foundation method for tulip petals on page 143 (D).

3 Use a cutting wheel to make two deep cuts on both sides of the petal to create five sections. Make multiple deep cuts towards the base of the petal in each section using fine scissors (E). See steps A–C on page 17 of Sugar Flower Foundations for more detailed images.

4 Place the petal on a foam pad and curl the cut edges by drawing a leaf shaping tool from the centre of the petal out towards the edges. Bend the wire of the petal to curve it outwards slightly at the base and in at the top. Use your fingers to shape the top of the petal and give it movement (F).

5 Brush the white section of the petal with White Satin dust food colour and the Poinsettia section of the petal with Poinsettia dust food colour. Dust the central vein and the base of the petal with a mixture of Leaf Green and Vine dust food colours.

6 Repeat steps 1–5 to make two more petals then attach them around the flower centre one by one using green floral tape. Use your fingers to overlap the top of the petals (G).

7 Repeat steps 1–6 to make three more petals for the outer layer; curl the cut edges at the top of the petals in towards the centre and the side edges outwards (H). Attach the outer petals to the flower one at a time over the joins between the inner petals using green floral tape (I).

Tip — Vary the shape and colour of the petals from flower to flower by using different ratios of Poinsettia and White SFP, and by curling the cut edges of the petals in different ways.

SEPALS

1 Combine White and Holly/Ivy SFP to create a light green paste.

2 Thinly roll out the light green SFP then thinly roll out some White SFP. Secure a 26-gauge white wire to the centre of the light green paste using edible glue then lay the White SFP on top. Secure the two pieces together by smoothing the paste with your finger. Cut out a sepal using the no. 8 cutter from SK Multi-Flower Cutter Set 2. Cut away 1cm (³/₈") from the bottom edge of the sepal using a cutting wheel.

3 With the light green side of the sepal facing upwards (this will be the outside), shape the sepal as in steps 2–4 of the parrot tulip petals. Curl the top edge of the petals in towards the centre and the side edges outwards (J).

4 Brush the green outside centre of the sepal with a mixture of Leaf Green and Holly/Ivy dust food colours and catch the edges with Poinsettia dust food colour (I).

5 Repeat steps 1–4 to make five sepals in total then attach them around the outer petals using green floral tape while they are semi-dry. Use your fingers to shape the sepals to fit nicely around the flower (K).

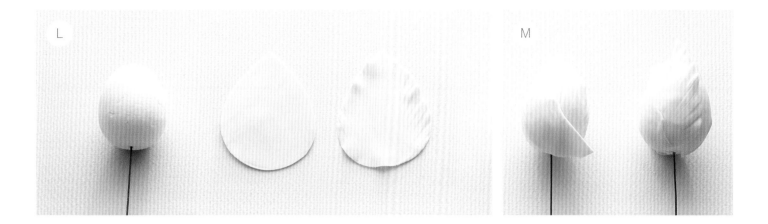

BUD

1 Make a base for the bud using the polystyrene flower base guide on page 19, a 22-gauge green wire and a 4cm x 5cm (1½" x 2") polystyrene ovoid.

2 Partially mix a small amount of Pale Green and White SFP and roll out the paste thinly. Cut out a petal using the no. 7 cutter from SK Multi-Flower Cutter Set 2, with the pointed end at the top. Texture the petal as in steps 2–3 of the foundation method for tulip petals on page 143 (L).

3 Attach the petal to the polystyrene bud base using edible glue: position the cut paste at the base of each petal around the wire so the petal fits around the shape of the polystyrene ovoid from bottom to top. Cut away any excess paste from both sides of the base of the petal.

4 Repeat steps 2–3 to make two more petals and attach them to the bud base, overlapping slightly at the top to hide the polystyrene base (M).

5 Thinly roll out some White and some Poinsettia SFP then secure them together, slightly overlapping. Cut out a petal with the colour ratio of your choice using the no. 8 cutter from SK Multi-Flower Cutter Set 2.

Texture and colour the petals as in steps 2–5 of the parrot tulip petals on page 159 and curl them as for the outer petals in step 7.

6 Repeat step 5 to make two more petals then attach them around the inner petals using edible glue, making sure the centre of each petal covers a join in the previous layer (N).

7 Make and attach three unwired sepals following the instructions for parrot tulip sepals on page 159 and using the no. 7 cutter from SK Multi-Flower Cutter Set 2 (O). After attaching the sepals and before they dry, very gently pinch the back of each sepal along the central vein to give the tulip a natural look.

STEM, LEAVES AND ASSEMBLY

Make the stem and leaves and assemble the tulip using the foundation methods on pages 143–144.

Fringed Tulip

Fringed tulips are one of the more recent tulip groups, with unusual fringed edges which create a ruffled effect. This group of tulips has many different kinds of colours and shapes as well. Some of them look like parrot tulips but I prefer this shape for the fringed tulip as its simple body enhances the delicate, lacy top edges.

EDIBLES

SK Sugar Florist Paste (SFP): Pale Green, Pale Yellow, Soft Lilac and White

SK Professional Dust Food Colours: Bulrush, Cyclamen, Daffodil, Holly/Ivy, Leaf Green and Vine

SK Quality Food Colour (QFC) Dust: Purple

SK Designer Pastel Dust Food Colour: Pale Lilac

SK Designer Bridal Satin Dust Food Colour: White Satin

EQUIPMENT

22-, 24- and 28-gauge green floral wires

26- and 30-gauge white floral wires

SK Multi-Flower Cutter Set 2: nos. 7 and 8

SK Multi-Flower Cutter Set 3: nos. 7, 8 and 9

Moss green floral tape

SK Great Impressions Corn Husk Textured Mat

ESSENTIAL EDIBLES AND EQUIPMENT (SEE PAGE 10)

FLOWER CENTRE

Make the flower centre using the foundation method for a tulip pistil and stamens on pages 142–143. Paint the anthers with a mixture of Bulrush dust food colour and clear alcohol in step 3 for the stamens.

PETALS

1 Knead a small amount of Soft Lilac SFP into White SFP to create a pale lilac paste.

2 Make three inner petals using steps 1–3 of the foundation method for tulip petals on page 143, 26-gauge white wires, the no. 7 petal cutter from SK Multi-Flower Cutter Set 2 and pale lilac SFP (A).

3 Use a cutting wheel to make 1–1.5cm (³/₈–⁵/₈") fine cuts down into the top edge of each petal (B). Curl the cuts outwards using a leaf shaping tool or roll them over a bamboo skewer using your finger (C).

4 Brush the entire surface of each petal lightly with White Satin dust food colour and the base of both sides with a mixture of Pale Lilac and Purple dust food colours (D).

5 Pinch together the bottom 1.5–2cm (⁵/₈–¾") of the petal around the wire. Make a cupped shape using step 5 of the foundation method for tulip petals on page 143.

6 Attach the petals overlapping around the flower centre one by one using green floral tape (E).

7 Repeat steps 2–5 to make the three outer petals but use the no. 8 cutter and cut away a 5mm (¼") 'V' shape from the base of the petal with a cutting wheel before veining the petals (F). Attach the outer petals to the flower one by one around the inner petals (G).

STEM, LEAVES AND ASSEMBLY

Make the stem and leaves and assemble the tulip using the foundation methods on pages 143–144.

Tip To make a bud or a just-opening flower, overlap the inner petals closely then attach the outer petals very closely around them.

Double-Flowered Tulip

Double-flowered tulips are usually defined as 'double early' or 'double late' depending on when they flower. With their extra petals and bowl-shaped blooms, they almost resemble peonies but still retain the charming look of tulips.

EDIBLES

SK Sugar Florist Paste (SFP): Pale Green,
Pale Yellow, Soft Peach and White

SK Professional Dust Food Colours:
Bulrush, Cyclamen, Daffodil, Edelweiss,
Fuchsia, Holly/Ivy, Leaf Green and Vine

EQUIPMENT

22-, 24- and 28-gauge green floral wires

26-, 28- and 30-gauge white floral wires

Orchard Products Five Petal Cutter:
F6 (6.5cm/2½")

SK Multi-Flower Cutter Set 2:
nos. 1, 4, 5, 6 and 7

SK Multi-Flower Cutter Set 3: nos. 7, 8 and 9

Moss green floral tape

SK Great Impressions Corn Husk Textured Mat

ESSENTIAL EDIBLES AND EQUIPMENT (SEE PAGE 10)

FLOWER CENTRE

Make the flower centre using the basic method for a tulip pistil and stamens on pages 142–143. Paint the anthers with a mixture of Bulrush dust food colour and clear alcohol in step 3 for the stamens.

PETALS

1 Thinly roll out some Soft Peach SFP and cut out a flower shape using the five petal cutter.

2 Make a small cut at the tip of the petal with the pointed end of the no. 1 cutter from SK Multi-Flower Cutter Set 2. Make a deeper cut on either side of the petal using a cutting wheel.

3 Vein the petals using a bamboo skewer (A). Use a leaf shaping tool to curl the edges inside the cut sides inwards and the sides of petals outwards.

4 Brush the petals with a mixture of Edelweiss and Fuchsia dust food colours.

5 Thread the flower shape up the wire of the flower centre and attach it with edible glue (B).

6 Thinly roll out some Soft Peach SFP and cut out three petals using the no. 4 cutter. Shape and colour the petals as in steps 2–4 (C). Attach them around the previous petals using edible glue so they are evenly spaced and the centre of each petal covers a join in the previous layer (D).

7 Mix White and Soft Peach SFP to make a pale peach paste. Cut out three wired petals using the large wired petals and leaves guide on page 19, 28-gauge white wires and the no. 5 cutter. Shape the petals as in steps 2–3 above then use your fingers to bend the wire inside each petal into a curve. Repeat to make three wired petals using the no. 6 cutter then make three wired petals using the no. 7 cutter and 26-gauge white wires (E, F).

8 Brush from the middle to the base of both the front and back of each petal with a mixture of Edelweiss and Fuchsia dust food colours. Brush areas of the petals with a little Vine dust food colour.

9 Attach the three small wired petals to the flower one by one around the inner petals using green floral tape then attach the three medium petals in the same way (G). Attach the three large wired petals in a more open position (H). Make sure each layer is evenly spaced and the centre of each petal covers a join in the previous layer.

Tip Finish the flower after the first layer of petals if you would like to make a bud, or after the second layer to make a just-opening flower.

STEM, LEAVES AND ASSEMBLY

Make the stem and leaves and assemble the tulip using the foundation methods on pages 143–144.

Peony

A traditional floral symbol of China, the peony is now a popular wedding flower around the world thanks to its large, showy blooms, delicately frilled petals and attractive variety of colours. There are more than 30 species of peony. Many of these are double flowers, meaning they have extra petals or flowers within flowers.

Peony Foundations

FLOWER CENTRE

Base

Flatten the top of a polystyrene ball flower base slightly with sandpaper. Wire it using the polystyrene flower base guide on page 19 and a 20-gauge green floral wire.

Use SK Multi-Flower Cutter Sets 1 and 2 to make all of the peony petals. The sizes needed are specified in this basic method and in the projects.

Central Petals

1 Use the no. 1 cutter from SK Multi-Flower Cutter Set 2 to cut out six petals. Soften the edges with a flower shaping tool (A).

2 Attach the petals, evenly spaced, to the top of the polystyrene ball using edible glue, positioning the pointed ends in the centre and tucking the edge of each petal under the previous one (B, C).

3 Make five petals as in step 1 using the no. 2 cutter. Attach the first petal around the ball with the round end facing towards the centre, making sure the top edge of the petal sits higher than the top of the ball. Pinch the base of the petal and fold the excess paste to one side (D, E). Glue the remaining four petals, overlapping, around the ball, tucking half of the final petal under the edge of the first (F).

4 Cut out five petals using the no. 5 cutter. Use the pointed end of the no. 1 cutter to cut a small notch out of the top of each petal. Soften the edges with a flower shaping tool (G).

5 Cup the petals by laying them over a 4cm (1½") polystyrene ball former. Fit the petal to the former from top to bottom and pull together the excess paste from both sides of the bottom of the petal into the centre. Fold the excess paste to one side and cut it away with fine scissors. Smooth the cut edges with your finger. Leave the petal to semi-dry on the former (H).

6 Attach the petals, one by one, around the flower, overlapping the edges and positioning them slightly higher than the previous row (I, J).

7 Cut out five petals using the no. 5 cutter. Use a cutting wheel to cut out a triangular section of paste from both sides of each petal.

8 Curl the top of the central part of the petal in towards the front, then turn the petal over and curl the side sections back using a leaf shaping tool (K). Shape the petal with your fingers and place it on a 4cm (1½") polystyrene ball former to semi-dry (L).

9 Attach the petals, one by one, at the base of flower centre with edible glue (M, N).

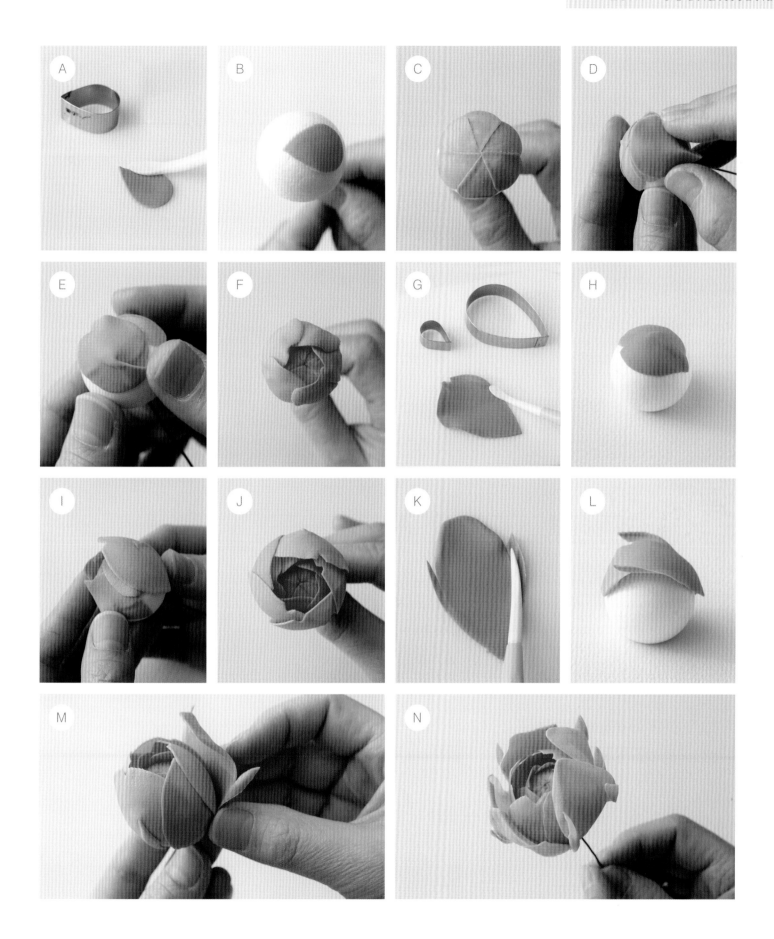

PETALS

Wired Petals

1 Cut out a petal using the large wired petals and leaves guide on page 19 with the size of the wire and cutter specified in the project.

2 Make small cuts in the top edge of the petal with the pointed end of the no. 1 cutter from SK Multi-Flower Cutter Set 2 (O).

3 Use a cutting wheel to cut out a triangular section of paste from each side of the petal (P).

4 Vein the petal with a bamboo skewer (Q).

5 Turn the petal over and place it on a foam pad. Soften the edges using a flower shaping tool. Curl back the side sections with a leaf shaping tool (R).

6 Curve the petal inwards by bending the wire slightly with your fingers (S).

Twisted Wired Petals

1 Make the petals as in steps 1–5 of the wired petals.

2 Pinch the base of the petal together (T). Curve the petal inwards by bending the wire slightly (U). Twist the top of the petal with your fingers (V).

BUDS

Closed Bud

1 Flatten the top of a 4cm (1½") polystyrene ball flower base slightly with sandpaper. Wire it using the polystyrene flower base guide on page 19 and a 20-gauge green wire.

2 Thinly roll out some SFP and cut out a petal using the no. 4 cutter from SK Multi-Flower Cutter Set 2. Attach the petal to the top of the flower base with edible glue. Fit the petal to the polystyrene ball from top to bottom and pull together the excess paste from both sides of the bottom of the petal into the centre. Fold the excess paste to one side and cut it away with fine scissors (W).

3 Thinly roll out some SFP and cut out three petals with the no. 6 cutter. Make small cuts in the top edge of the petal with the pointed end of the no. 1 cutter. Vein the petals with a bamboo skewer. Turn the petals over, place them on a foam pad and soften the edges with a flower shaping tool.

4 Attach the petals evenly around the flower base, positioning them as close as possible to the top of the bud. Cut away the excess paste at the bottoms of the petals as in step 2 (X).

5 Thinly roll out some SFP and cut out three petals with the no. 7 cutter. Make a small cut at the top edge on one side of the petal with the pointed end of the no. 1 petal cutter. Adjust the curve of the petal with a cutting wheel if necessary. Vein the petals using a Corn Husk texture mat.

6 Brush the edges of the petals with Vine dust food colour.

7 Cup the petals on a 4cm (1½") ball former, with the veined side on the outside. Pull and cut away the excess paste as in step 2. Attach the petals evenly around the base of the bud (Y).

8 Make three long, narrow calyx sepals as in steps 6–8 of the calyx overleaf. Tape them to the bud upside down.

Opening Bud

1 Begin the opening bud as in steps 1–4 of the closed bud.

2 Thinly roll out some SFP and cut out three petals using the no. 6 cutter and three petals using the no. 7 cutter.

3 Make small cuts in the top edge of each petal using the pointed end of the no. 1 cutter. Widen the petals by rolling them out with a CelStick then vein them using a bamboo skewer.

4 Cup the petals on a 5cm (2") polystyrene ball former with the veined side on the outside.

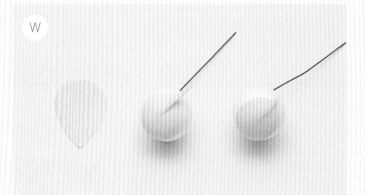

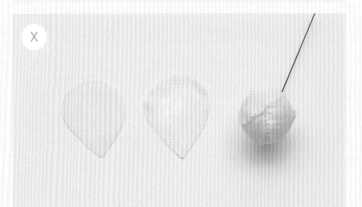

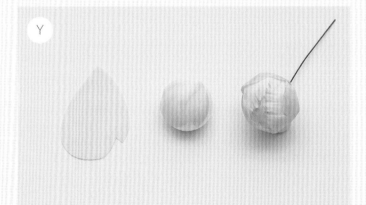

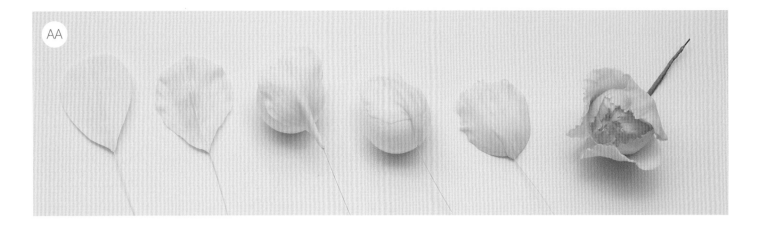

5 Attach the three petals made with the no. 6 cutter evenly around the flower centre. Position them slightly lower than the previous petals, with the centre of each petal covering a join in the previous row. Attach the three larger petals at the base of the bud in the same way (Z, see previous page).

6 Cut out three wired petals using the large wired petals and leaves guide on page 19, 26-gauge white wires and the no. 7 cutter.

7 Shape the petals as in step 3 for the opening bud (see previous page), veining them on both sides. Frill the edges using a bone tool.

8 Cup the petals loosely on a 5cm (2") polystyrene ball former.

9 Brush the outside base of each petal with dust food colour.

10 Whilst the petals are only semi-dry, tape them evenly around the bud, with the centre of each petal covering a join in the previous row. Shape the petals with your fingers to make them look more natural (AA).

11 Make calyces following the calyx instructions. Tape them at the bottom of the bud upside down.

CALYX

1 Cut out three wired calyx sepals using the small wired petals and leaves guide on page 19, Pale Green SFP, the no. 4 cutter from SK Multi-Flower Cutter Set 1, with the most pointed end at the top, and 28-gauge green wires.

2 Vein the calyx sepals with a Corn Husk texture mat. Curl the top of the sepals inwards using a flower shaping tool then pinch the base.

3 Dust both sides of the calyx sepals with a mixture of Holly/Ivy and Leaf Green dust food colours, then catch the edges with Cyclamen (AB).

4 Tape the calyx sepals evenly around the final layer of flower petals one by one.

5 Repeat step 1 to cut out three narrow wired sepals approximately 5cm (2") in length (or longer for larger flowers) using a cutting wheel.

6 Use a leaf shaping tool to mark a line down the centre of the narrower sepals and two angled lines along either side. Soften the edges of the sepals with a flower shaping tool.

7 Dust the calyx sepals as in step 4.

AC

ASSEMBLY

Add a leaf stem to the flower stem, taping them together a few centimetres under the base of the leaf. Dust the stems with a mixture of Holly/Ivy and Leaf Green dust food colours, adding Cyclamen where the stem joins with leaves and calyces.

8 Tape the sepals upside-down in between the previous layer of calyx petals.

LEAVES

1 Cut out three wired leaves using Pale Green SFP and 28-gauge green wires. Use a larger cutter for the central leaf and a smaller cutter for the two side leaves, both from SK Multi-Flower Cutter Set 3. Make sure that the most pointed end of the cutter is at the base of the leaf and they are in proportion with the flower head.

2 Soften the edges of the leaves with a flower shaping tool. Use a leaf shaping tool to mark the central vein and two asymmetrical angled veins on either side.

3 Dust the leaves with a mixture of Holly/Ivy and Leaf Green dust food colours then catch the edges with Cyclamen.

4 Tape each wire individually with brown floral tape. Tape the three leaves together with the two smaller leaves on either side and slightly below the large leaf. A single leaf can also be used.

5 Coat the leaves with confectioners' glaze to give them a shiny finish.

STEM

If the peony needs a stronger stem to support the flower, add an 18- or 20-gauge wire beneath the flower head and tape down the stem with green floral tape.

Chinese Peony

Native to central and eastern Asia, *Paeonia lactiflora* has provided hundreds of cultivated varieties. The Chinese peony looks beautiful if you make it in pure white or deep, purplish pink as well.

EDIBLES

SK Sugar Florist Paste (SFP): Pale Green,
Soft Lilac and White

SK Professional Dust Food Colours:
Cyclamen, Holly/Ivy, Leaf Green, Lilac and Vine

SK Designer Pollen Dust Food Colour:
Pale Golden

SK Designer Bridal Satin Dust Food Colour:
White Satin

EQUIPMENT

26- and 28-gauge white floral wires

20-, 28- and 30-gauge green floral wires

Brown, green and white floral tape

Medium matt white pointed-head stamens

SK Multi-Flower Cutter Set 1: no. 4

SK Multi-Flower Cutter Set 2: nos. 1, 4, 6 and 7

SK Multi-Flower Cutter Set 3: nos. 4 and 5

4cm (1½") polystyrene ball

4cm and 5cm (1½" and 2") polystyrene
ball formers

SK Great Impressions Corn Husk Textured Mat

ESSENTIAL EDIBLES AND EQUIPMENT (SEE PAGE 10)

FLOWER CENTRE

1 Form a 2cm (¾") long teardrop shape of Pale Green SFP using your finger and thumb. Place the teardrop on a foam pad and cup the thinner top end using a bone tool. Brush a hooked 30-gauge green wire with edible glue and insert it into the base of the shape.

2 Repeat step 1 to make four more pistils. Dust the main body of each pistil with Holly/Ivy dust food colour and dust the tops with Cyclamen (A). Leave the pistils to semi-dry.

3 Use green floral tape to fix the five pistils together around a central 20-gauge hooked green wire (B).

4 Cut 10 pointed-head stamens to 4cm (1½") lengths from the base of the head. Tape the trimmed stamens together at the same height using white floral tape (C). Paint the top of the filaments with a mixture of Cyclamen dust food colour and clear alcohol. Brush edible glue on the anthers and cover them with Pale Golden pollen (D).

5 Repeat step 4 to make eight more bunches of stamens. Secure the stamen bunches around the pistils with green floral tape: first tape three bunches equally spaced around the pistil then tape two bunches between each secured bunch (E).

PETALS

1 For the first layer, make five petals using the foundation method for twisted wired peony petals on page 176, Soft Lilac SFP, the no. 6 petal cutter from SK Multi-Flower Cutter Set 2 and 28-gauge white wires (F).

2 Dust the whole surface of each petal lightly with White Satin dust food colour and brush Lilac dust food colour at the base of each petal.

3 Place each petal in a ring of tissue paper to hold its shape until semi-dry (G).

4 Tape the petals one by one around the flower centre using green floral tape, spacing them evenly.

5 For the second layer, make five petals using the foundation method for wired peony petals on page 176, omitting step 3 for cutting sections from either side of the petals. Use the no. 6 petal cutter and 28-gauge white wires. Use a bone tool instead of a flower shaping tool to frill the edge of the petals in step 5 (H).

6 Dust the petals with White Satin and Lilac dust food colours (I). Place each petal in a ring of tissue paper to hold its shape until semi-dry.

7 Use green floral tape to fix the petals around the flower one by one, with the centre of each petal covering a join in the previous row (J).

8 For the third layer, repeat step 5 to make six petals using the no. 6 cutter and 26-gauge white wires. Before veining the petals, widen them by rolling out the paste on either side of the wire using a CelStick (K). Dust and attach the petals as in steps 6–7.

9 For the fourth layer, make and attach six petals using the no. 7 petal cutter, 26-gauge white wires and the same process as in step 8 (L, M).

CALYX

Make and attach the calyx using the foundation method for a peony calyx on pages 178–179.

BUDS

Make closed and opening buds using the foundation method for peony buds on pages 177–178.

LEAVES

Make and attach the leaves using the foundation method for peony leaves on page 179, nos. 4 and 5 petal cutters from SK Multi-Flower Cutter Set 3 and 28-gauge green wires.

STEM AND ASSEMBLY

Finish the flower following the foundation methods for a peony stem and assembly on page 179.

Anemone Peony

The Anemone type of peony is like the Chinese flower except for the stamens: they don't have any anthers and the filaments look like a cluster of narrow, curved petals. I like to use wafer paper for the stamens as they are long and thin. It makes them less fragile and is quicker than making lots of stamens from flower paste.

EDIBLES

SK Sugar Florist Paste (SFP): Pale Green, Pale Pink and White

SK Professional Dust Food Colours: Cyclamen, Holly/Ivy, Leaf Green, Rose and Vine

SK Quality Food Colour (QFC) Dust: Pink

SK Designer Bridal Satin Dust Food Colour: White Satin

SK Edible Wafer Paper: White

EQUIPMENT

24-, 26- and 28-gauge white floral wires

20-, 28- and 30-gauge green floral wires

Brown and green floral tape

SK Multi-Flower Cutter Set 1: nos. 4, 9 and 10

SK Multi-Flower Cutter Set 2: nos. 1, 4, 6, 7 and 8

SK Multi-Flower Cutter Set 3: nos. 4 and 5

4cm, 6cm, 7cm and 8cm (1½", 2³/₈", 2³/₄" and 3¹/₈") polystyrene ball formers

4cm (1½") polystyrene balls

SK Great Impressions Corn Husk Textured Mat

ESSENTIAL EDIBLES AND EQUIPMENT (SEE PAGE 10)

Tip Be careful to not brush too much water on the wafer paper as this can cause the sheet to dissolve.

FLOWER CENTRE

1 Make three 2.5cm (1") long teardrop shapes from Pale Green SFP using your finger and thumb. Thin the tips of the teardrops and bend them outwards slightly. Insert a glued, hooked 30-gauge green wire into the base of each shape. Brush Holly/Ivy dust food colour around the base of each pistil and Cyclamen at the top. Fix the three pistils together with green floral tape whilst semi-dry so that they fit together nicely (A).

2 To make the stamens, cut a sheet of wafer paper into an 18cm x 14cm (7" x 5½") rectangle then divide it into three along the longer side, making one piece 7cm (2¾") wide, one 6cm (2¼") wide and one 5cm (2") wide. Use a pencil to draw a line 1cm (³/₈") up from the bottom long edge of each piece then make marks at 1cm (³/₈") intervals along each line. Cut triangles down to the marked points along the length of the paper (B). Repeat with another sheet of wafer paper cut into two 7cm x 14cm (2¾" x 5½") rectangles.

3 Brush a very small amount of cooled, boiled water over one side of each of the wafer paper pieces using a small paintbrush. Leave for approximately 30 minutes until the pointed ends have curled forwards.

4 Cut one of the 7cm (2¾") wide wafer paper strips into thirds. Cut each of the pointed triangles on each strip in half (C).

5 Brush a little water along the base of one of the prepared stamen pieces from step 4 (D). Place a 28-gauge white wire in the centre. Concertina fold the base of the strip around the wire and press it together tightly to secure (E). Use small scissors to cut away the excess paper from the base of the stamens diagonally on both sides of the wire (F). Repeat to wire the remaining two prepared stamen pieces.

6 Repeat steps 4–5 to make stamen pieces with the remaining 5cm, 6cm and 7cm (2", 2³/₈" and 2¾") wafer paper stamen strips, without adding a wire (G).

7 Attach an unwired 7cm (2¾") stamen piece to either side of a wired stamen piece using a little cooled, boiled water or edible glue (H, I). Repeat with the remaining two wired stamen pieces.

8 Dust the lower halves of the wired stamens with a mixture of Pink and Rose dust food colours.

9 Use green floral tape to attach the three stamen sections evenly around the pistils (J).

10 Dust the 5cm and 6cm (2" and 2³/₈") stamen pieces as in step 8 then attach them in the gaps using a little cooled, boiled water or edible glue (K, L).

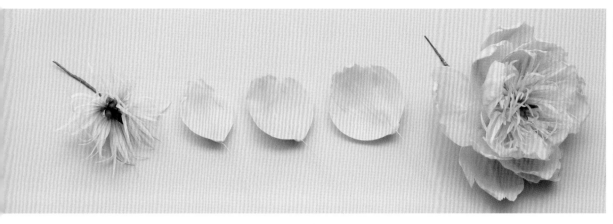
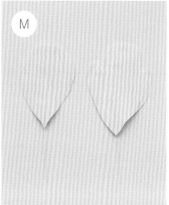

PETALS

1 Cut out and texture five petals using steps 1–5 of the foundation method for wired peony petals on page 176, Pale Pink SFP, the no. 8 cutter from SK Multi-Flower Cutter Set 2 and 26-gauge white wires (M).

2 Brush White Satin dust food colour lightly over the surface of each petal and dust the bases with a mixture of Rose and Pink.

3 Bring the two cut side sections to the inside of the petal to make the upper part of the petal curve inwards. Cup each petal on a 6cm (2³/₈") polystyrene ball former using steps 3–6 of the foundation method for wired cupped rose petals on page 33 (N).

4 Whilst the petals are semi-dry, tape three of them evenly around the flower centre then tape the remaining two behind the first petals with green floral tape.

5 Repeat steps 1–4 to make and attach a second layer of five petals using the no. 9 cutter from SK Multi-Flower Cutter Set 1, 24-gauge white wires and a 7cm (2³/₄") polystyrene ball former (O).

6 Repeat steps 1–4 to make and attach a third layer of five petals using the no. 10 cutter from SK Multi-Flower Cutter Set 1, 24-gauge white wires and an 8cm (3¹/₈") polystyrene ball former (P).

CALYX

Make and attach the calyx using the foundation method for a peony calyx on pages 178–179. Tape a hooked 20-gauge green wire to the stem to strengthen it.

BUDS

Make closed and opening buds using the foundation method for peony buds on pages 177–178.

LEAVES

Make and attach the leaves using the foundation method for peony leaves on page 179, nos. 4 and 5 cutters from SK Multi-Flower Cutter Set 3 and 28-gauge green wires.

STEM AND ASSEMBLY

Finish the flower following the foundation methods for a peony stem and assembly on page 179.

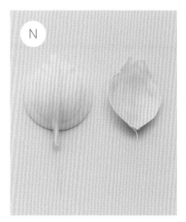
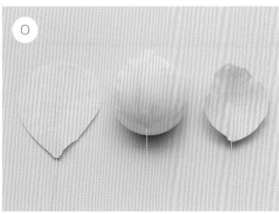
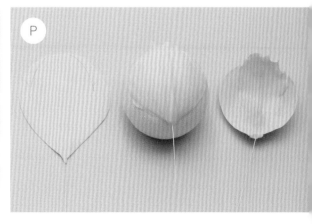

Peony Rose

The remaining three flowers in this section are examples of double peonies, where the stamens and sometimes stigmas have transformed into extra petals. This peony rose is a large sugar flower, measuring nearly 20cm (8") in diameter. If you would like to make it slightly smaller, omit step 7 for the wired petals. You may also wish to reduce the number of additional petals.

EDIBLES

SK Sugar Florist Paste (SFP): Pale Green, Pale Pink and White

SK Designer Bridal Satin Dust Food Colour: White Satin

SK Quality Food Colour (QFC) Dust: Pink

SK Professional Dust Food Colours: Cyclamen, Holly/Ivy, Leaf Green, Rose and Vine

EQUIPMENT

24-, 26- and 28-gauge white floral wires

20- and 28-gauge green floral wires

SK Multi-Flower Cutter Set 1: nos. 4 and 9

SK Multi-Flower Cutter Set 2: nos. 1, 2, 4, 5, 6, 7 and 8

SK Multi-Flower Cutter Set 3: nos. 4 and 5

Brown and green floral tape

3cm and 4cm (1$\frac{1}{8}$" and 1$\frac{1}{2}$") polystyrene balls

4cm, 5cm and 6cm (1$\frac{1}{2}$", 2" and 2$\frac{3}{8}$") polystyrene ball formers

SK Great Impressions Corn Husk Textured Mat

ESSENTIAL EDIBLES AND EQUIPMENT (SEE PAGE 10)

FLOWER CENTRE

Make the base and central petals using the foundation methods on page 174 with 3cm and 4cm (1¹/₈" and 1¹/₂") polystyrene balls and Pale Pink SFP.

PETALS

Wired Petals

1 Make five petals using the foundation method for wired peony petals on page 176, Pale Pink SFP partially mixed with White SFP, the no. 6 petal cutter from SK Multi-Flower Cutter Set 2 and 28-gauge white wires (A).

2 Brush the surface of each petal lightly with White Satin dust food colour. Brush a mixture of Pink and Rose dust food colours on the edges and central veins of the petals.

3 Use green floral tape to attach the petals one by one around the flower, with the centre of each petal covering a join in the previous layer.

4 Roll out some Pale Pink SFP and cut out a 1.5cm x 2cm (⁵/₈" x ³/₄") rectangle. Wrap this belt of paste around the wire underneath the first layer of wired petals and secure it with edible glue (B).

5 For the second layer, make six petals as in steps 1–2 using 26-gauge wires. Make three using the no. 6 petal cutter and three using the no. 7 petal cutter from SK Multi-Flower Cutter Set 2 (C). Attach the petals by first taping the three larger ones evenly underneath the belt of paste and then taping the smaller petals in the gaps between them (D).

6 Make six petals as in step 5 for the third layer, this time widening them by rolling out the paste on either side of the wire with a CelStick after cutting out the foundation petal shapes. Make three petals using the no. 7 petal cutter (E) and three using a no. 8 petal cutter (F). Tape the three smaller petals behind the smaller ones in the previous layer of petals then tape the larger petals in the gaps between them.

7 For the fourth layer, cut out and attach four petals made with the no. 9 petal cutter from SK Multi-Flower Cutter Set 1 and 24-gauge white wires (G, H).

Additional petals

1 Thinly roll out some of the mixed paste used for the wired petals. Cut out several petals using the no. 6 and no. 7 petal cutters from SK Multi-Flower Cutter Set 2.

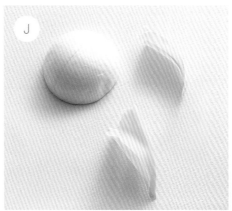

2 Vein the petals using a bamboo skewer and frill the edges with a bone tool. Bend a curve in the petals from the base up to the centre (I) then leave them to firm on 5cm or 6cm (2" or 2³/₈") polystyrene ball formers until semi-dry (J).

3 Attach the additional petals in between the second, third and fourth layers with edible glue, ensuring that the flower is nicely balanced (K).

Tip As a finishing touch, brush Vine or a mixture of Pink and Rose dust food colours at the bottom of some petals to bring them to life.

CALYX

Make and attach the calyx using the foundation method for a peony calyx on pages 178–179.

BUDS

Make closed and opening buds using the foundation method for peony buds on pages 177–178.

LEAVES

Make and attach the leaves using the foundation method for peony leaves on page 179, nos. 4 and 5 petal cutters from SK Multi-Flower Cutter Set 3 and 28-gauge green wires.

STEM AND ASSEMBLY

Finish the flower following the foundation methods for a peony stem and assembly on page 179.

Cupped Double Peony

This double flower is similar to the peony rose except, as the title suggests, the petals are more curved and appear to cup the centre. If you would like to make frilled petals for this flower, pleat each petal and cup it on a polystyrene ball former, making sure there is no excess paste at the bottom (see the top right image on page 203).

EDIBLES

SK Sugar Florist Paste (SFP): Pale Green, Pale Pink and White

SK Professional Dust Food Colours: Cyclamen, Holly/Ivy, Rose, Leaf Green and Vine

SK Quality Food Colour (QFC) Dust: Pink

SK Designer Bridal Satin Dust Food Colour: White Satin

EQUIPMENT

18-, 20- and 28-gauge green floral wires

24- and 28-gauge white floral wires

SK Multi-Flower Cutter Set 1: nos. 4, 9 and 10

SK Multi-Flower Cutter Set 2: nos. 1, 4, 5, 6, 7 and 8

SK Multi-Flower Cutter Set 3: nos. 4 and 5

Brown and green floral tape

4cm (1½") polystyrene balls

4cm, 5cm, 6cm, 7cm, 8cm and 10cm (1¹/₂", 2", 2³/₈", 2 ³/₄", 3¹/₈" and 4") polystyrene ball formers

SK Great Impressions Corn Husk Textured Mat

ESSENTIAL EDIBLES AND EQUIPMENT (SEE PAGE 10)

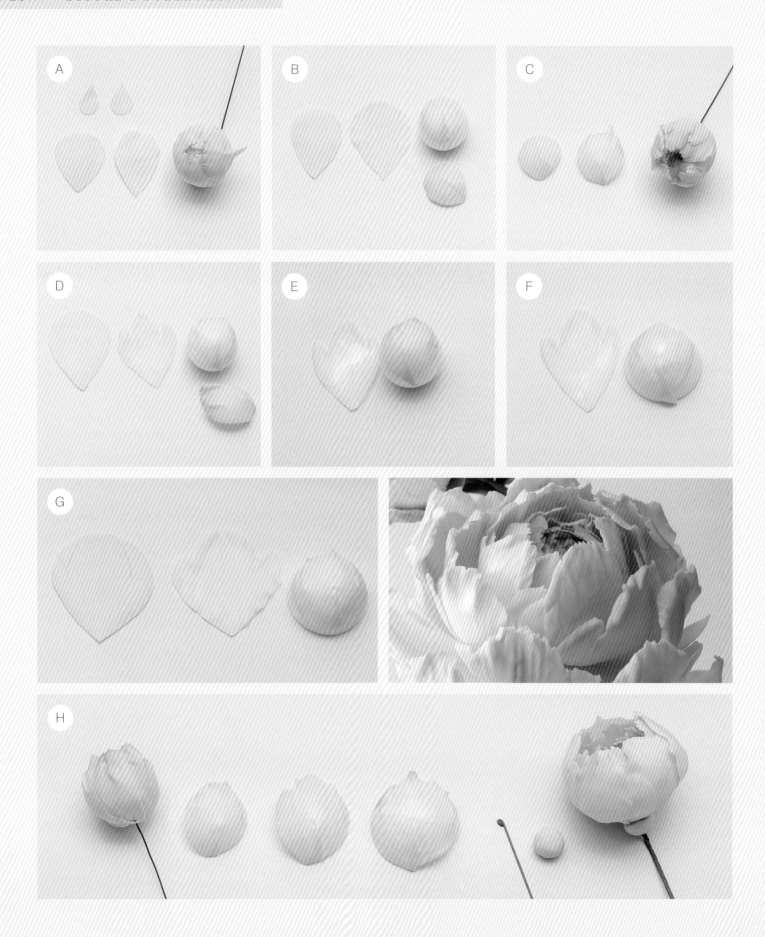

FLOWER CENTRE

1 Make the flower base using a 4cm (1½") polystyrene ball and the foundation method for a peony flower base on page 174.

2 Use steps 1–3 of the foundation method for central petals on page 174 with Pale Pink SFP. In step 3 use the no. 4 petal cutter from SK Multi-Flower Cutter Set 2 to cut out the petal shapes. Use the pointed end of the no. 1 cutter to cut out small notches at the top of the petals before shaping and attaching them to the flower centre (A).

3 Brush with a mixture of Pink and Rose dust food colours.

PETALS

Inner Petals

1 Mix some White and Pale Pink SFP to make a very light pink paste. Thinly roll out some of the light pink paste and cut out five petals using the no. 5 petal cutter from SK Multi-Flower Cutter Set 2.

2 Make small cuts at the top edge of the petal with the pointed end of the no. 1 petal cutter. Vein the petal with a bamboo skewer. Turn the petal over, place it on a foam pad and soften the edges using a flower shaping tool.

3 Brush the surface of each petal lightly with White Satin dust food colour. Brush a mixture of Pink and Rose dust food colours in places at the edges.

4 Place the petals, one by one, over a 4cm (1½") polystyrene ball former, veined side up. Fit the petal to the former from top to bottom and pull together the excess paste from both sides of the bottom of the petal into the centre. Fold the excess paste to one side and cut it away with fine scissors. Smooth the cut edges with your finger. Leave the petal on the former until semi-dry (B).

5 Attach the petals evenly around the flower centre using edible glue at the base, with the centre of each petal covering a join in the previous layer of petals (C).

6 Repeat steps 1–5 to make and attach the second layer of five petals using the no. 6 petal cutter and a 4cm (1½") polystyrene ball former. Before veining the petals, use a cutting wheel to cut out a section of paste from the edges on both sides. Use a leaf shaping tool to curve these edges before dusting the petals (D).

7 For the third layer, make and attach five petals as in step 6 using the no. 7 petal cutter and a 5cm (2") polystyrene ball former (E).

8 Make and attach five petals as in step 6 using the no. 8 petal cutter and a 6cm (2³⁄₈") polystyrene ball former for the fourth layer of petals (F).

9 For the fifth layer, make and attach five petals as in step 6 using the no. 9 petal cutter from SK Multi-Flower Cutter Set 1 and a 6cm (2³⁄₈") polystyrene ball former (G).

10 Tape an 18-gauge hooked green wire to the wire of the flower centre to strengthen the stem. Roll a 2cm (¾") ball of Pale Pink SFP, thread it up the wire and secure it under the petals using edible glue (H).

Outer Petals

1 Cut out and texture five petals using steps 1–5 of the foundation method for wired peony petals on page 176, very light pink SFP, the no. 9 petal cutter from SK Multi-Flower Cutter Set 1 and 24-gauge white wires.

2 Brush White Satin dust food colour lightly over the surface of each petal and dust the base of each petal with a mixture of Rose and Pink.

3 Cup each petal on a 7cm (2¾") polystyrene ball former, veined side down, using steps 4–7 of the foundation method for wired cupped rose petals on page 33 (I).

4 When the petals are only semi-dry, tape them evenly around the flower using green floral tape.

5 Roll a 2cm (¾") ball of Pale Pink SFP, thread it up the wire and secure it under the petals using edible glue.

6 Repeat steps 1–4 to make and attach five petals using the no. 10 petal cutter and an 8cm (3¹/₈") polystyrene ball former (J).

7 For the final layer, make and attach five petals as in steps 1–4 using the no. 10 petal cutter and a 10cm (4") polystyrene ball former, making sure the centre of each petal covers a join in the previous layer.

CALYX

Make and attach the calyx using the foundation method for a peony calyx on pages 178–179, the no. 4 petal cutter from SK Multi-Flower Cutter Set 1 and 28-gauge green wires.

BUDS

Make closed and opening buds using the foundation method for peony buds on pages 177–178. Vary the sizes of the buds by varying the number of layers of petals.

LEAVES

Make and attach the leaves using the foundation method for peony leaves on page 179, the nos. 4 and 5 petal cutters from SK Multi-Flower Cutter Set 3 and 28-gauge green wires.

STEM AND ASSEMBLY

Finish the flower following the foundation methods for a peony stem and assembly on page 179.

Temari Peony

The outer guard petals are longer and more prominent in this shape of peony, which is more commonly known as a 'bomb' flower form. I think of the shape as being like a temari, a traditional Japanese children's toy made by twining silk threads around a hand-sized ball. Arrange the penultimate layer of petals to give the flower a spherical form and it will look beautiful.

EDIBLES

SK Sugar Florist Paste (SFP): Pale Green and White

SK Designer Bridal Satin Dust Food Colour: White Satin

SK Professional Dust Food Colours: Cyclamen, Holly/Ivy, Leaf Gree, Rose and Vine

EQUIPMENT

26- and 28-gauge white floral wires

20- and 28-gauge green floral wires

SK Multi-Flower Cutter Set 1: nos. 4 and 9

SK Multi-Flower Cutter Set 2: nos. 1, 2, 4, 5, 6 and 7

SK Multi-Flower Cutter Set 3: nos. 4 and 5

Brown and green floral tape

3cm and 4cm (1^1/$_8$" and 1^1/$_2$") polystyrene balls

4cm and 5cm (1^1/$_2$" and 2") polystyrene ball formers

SK Great Impressions Corn Husk Textured Mat

ESSENTIAL EDIBLES AND EQUIPMENT (SEE PAGE 10)

FLOWER CENTRE

1 Make the base for the flower centre using the foundation method for a peony flower base on page 174 and a 3cm (1¹/₈") polystyrene ball.

2 Follow steps 1–3 of the foundation method for central peony petals on page 174 using White SFP. In step 3, use the no. 4 cutter from SK Multi-Flower Cutter Set 2 to cut out the petal shapes. Use the pointed end of the no. 1 cutter to cut out small notches at the top of the petals before shaping and attaching them to the flower centre (A).

3 Thinly roll out some White SFP and cut out six petals using the no. 5 cutter. Use a cutting wheel to make three deep, V-shaped cuts down from the top edge of the petals. Vein the petals with a bamboo skewer then make a pleat in the centre of each one running from the base to the middle of the petal. Place the petals over a 4cm (1½") polystyrene ball former and leave until semi-dry (B).

4 Attach the petals evenly around the flower centre. Roll a small ball of White SFP, place it on a foam pad and press a ball tool into it to give it a cupped shape. Thread the cupped ball up the wire of the flower centre and secure it against the base of the flower centre using edible glue (C).

PETALS

1 Make six petals using the foundation method for twisted wired peony petals on page 176, White SFP, the no. 6 cutter from SK Multi-Flower Cutter Set 2 and 28-gauge white wires (D).

2 Brush the surface of each petal lightly with White Satin dust food colour and dust a little Vine at the base.

3 Use green floral tape to fix the petals evenly around the flower centre, making sure the centre of each petal covers a join in the previous row.

4 Roll a small sausage of White SFP in the palms of your hands and wrap it around the base of the petals, securing it with edible glue (E).

Make six petals using the foundation method for wired peony petals on page 176, White SFP, the no. 6 cutter from SK Multi-Flower Cutter Set 2 and 28-gauge white wires (F). Repeat steps 2 and 3.

5 Make six petals using the foundation method for wired peony petals on page 176. Use White SFP, the no. 7 cutter from SK Multi-Flower Cutter Set 2 and 26-gauge white wires (G, H). Repeat step 2 to dust the petals then tape them around the previous row of petals.

6 Make six petals using the foundation method for twisted wired peony petals on page 176, White SFP, the no. 7 cutter from SK Multi-Flower Cutter Set 2 and 26-gauge white wires (I). Repeat step 2 to dust the petals then tape them around the previous row of petals (J).

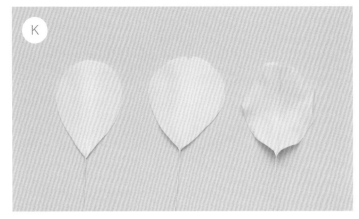

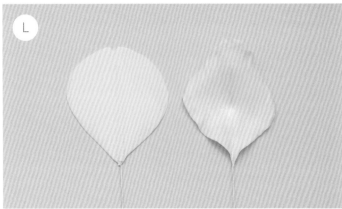

7 Thinly roll out some White SFP and cut out five wired petals using the no. 7 cutter and 26-gauge white wires as in step 6. Widen the petals by rolling out the paste on either side of the wire using a CelStick. Use the pointed end of the no. 7 cutter to cut away a small triangle from the tip of each petal. Finish shaping the petals following steps 4–6 of the foundation method for wired peony petals on page 176. Dust and attach the petals to the flower as in steps 2–3 (K).

8 Follow step 7 to make and attach five petals for the final layer using the no. 9 cutter from SK Multi-Flower Cutter Set 1 and 26-gauge white wires, but don't widen the petals this time. Use the pointed end of the no. 7 petal cutter to cut a small triangle from the tip of each petal as for the previous layer (L, M).

9 Thinly roll out some White SFP and cut out approximately eight petals with each of the no. 4 and no. 5 cutters from SK Multi-Flower Cutter Set 2. Cut and shape the petals following step 3 for the flower centre on the previous page.

10 Once they are semi-dry, use edible glue to attach the pleated petals made with cutter no. 4 in the spaces between the petals made in steps 4 and 5. Attach the pleated petals made with cutter no. 5 between the outer three layers of petals, ensuring the shape of the flower is balanced (N).

11 Brush a small amount of Rose dust food colour over the top edge of some of the petals to finish the flower.

CALYX

Make and attach the calyx using the foundation method for a peony calyx on pages 178–179.

BUDS

Closed Buds

Follow the foundation method for closed peony buds on page 177.

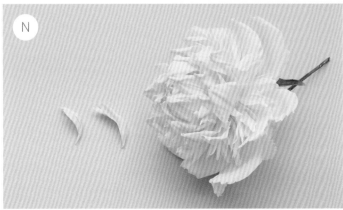

Opening Buds

1 Make the base following the foundation method for a peony flower centre base on page 174.

2 Follow steps 1–3 of the foundation method for central peony petals on page 174 to add the first layer of petals.

3 Add a second layer of petals using steps 6–10 of the foundation method for opening peony buds on page 178.

4 Brush a small amount of Rose dust food colour over the top edge of some of the petals.

5 Attach a calyx to the bud using the foundation method for a peony calyx on pages 178–179.

LEAVES

Make and attach the leaves using the foundation method for peony leaves on page 179, the no. 4 and no. 5 petal cutters from SK Multi-Flower Cutter Set 3 and 28-gauge green wires.

STEM AND ASSEMBLY

Finish the flower following the foundation methods for a peony stem and assembly on page 179.

Flower Index

Squires Kitchen, UK
Squires House
3 Waverley Lane
Farnham
Surrey
GU9 8BB
+44 (0)1252 260 260
squires-shop.com

Squires Kitchen International School, UK
The Grange
Hones Yard
Farnham
Surrey
GU9 8BB
+44 (0)1252 260 262
squires-school.co.uk

OTHER BOOKS BY NAOMI YAMAMOTO

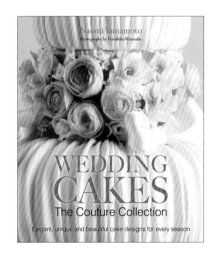 

  B. Dutton Publishing is an award-winning publisher of cake decorating, chocolate and sugarcraft titles. To find out more about our books, follow us at **facebook.com/bduttonpublishing** and **twitter.com/bduttonbooks**.